Library of
Davidson College

Worldwatch Paper 89

National Security:
The Economic and
Environmental Dimensions

Michael Renner

May 1989

The Worldwatch Institute is an independent, nonprofit research organization created to analyze and to focus attention on global problems. Directed by Lester R. Brown, Worldwatch is funded by private foundations and United Nations organizations. Worldwatch papers are written for a worldwide audience of decision makers, scholars, and the general public.

National Security:
The Economic and
Environmental Dimensions

Michael Renner

Library of
Davidson College

Worldwatch Paper 89
May 1989

Sections of this paper may be reproduced in magazines and newspapers with acknowledgment to the Worldwatch Institute. The views expressed in this paper are those of the author and do not necessarily represent those of the Worldwatch Institute and its directors, officers, or staff, or of funding organizations.

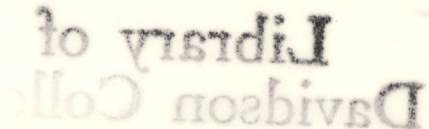

© Worldwatch Institute, 1989
Library of Congress Catalog Card Number 89-50738
ISBN 0-916468-90-9

Printed on Recycled Paper

Table of Contents

Introduction 5
A World at War 7
The Drain of a Permanent War Economy 14
Armaments and Underdevelopment 25
Environment and Security 29
From Military to Environmental Alliances 38
From National to Global Security 47
Conclusion 62
Notes 65

Introduction

Over the course of history, national security has come to be defined almost exclusively in military terms—the ability to deter or repel outside aggression. Because the need to safeguard the homeland from external threat has seldom been questioned, particularly since World War II governments have been able to invoke national security to justify the maintenance of increasingly large standing armed forces, the deployment of ever-newer weapons systems, frequent intervention in the affairs of weaker nations, and even the systematic violation of human rights at home.

It is becoming clear, however, that this growing reliance on force is actually reducing national security. In the age of weapons of mass destruction "the capacity to defend in order to deter [an attacker] has been replaced by the capability to destroy massively without the ability to defend," according to Gene Sharp, director of the Program on Nonviolent Sanctions in Conflict and Defense at Harvard University. Thus, the accumulation of weapons and the growth of military power is more likely to diminish the security of an opponent than to add to a nation's own security. In fact, the proliferation of strategic nuclear weapons has brought every human being within the compass of instant destruction. Competitive national security policies have yielded international insecurity.[1]

At the same time, the pursuit of military power is undermining the economies of rich and poor countries alike. A large and lasting

---

I would like to thank Susan Norris for her dedicated production assistance, and Meri McCoy-Thompson and Susan Fine for their able research support. I am grateful to Greg Bischak, Hal Harvey, and my colleagues at Worldwatch for their valuable review comments, and to Robert Johansen for having inspired much of this work. Any remaining errors or misinterpretations are solely my responsibility.

resource drain toward the military undermines economic security by retarding civilian research and development, slowing productivity growth, detracting from international competitiveness, and contributing to indebtedness. It can be said that Japan is the true victor in the cold war, partly a result of the fact that since 1945 it has invested a meager 1 percent of its gross national product in the military while the superpowers were engaged in an all-out arms race.

Perhaps worst, governments preoccupied with security threats of military origin have ignored the perils of environmental degradation. But national security is a meaningless concept if it does not include the preservation of livable conditions within a country—or on the planet as a whole. Increasingly, countries are finding their security undermined by environmental threats emanating from other nations, such as pollutants flowing across their frontiers through the air or water, or cataclysmic floods unleashed by denuded watersheds far from their borders. On a global scale, climate change, ozone depletion, deterioration of the agricultural base, and deforestation are formidable challenges to the safety and well-being of the entire race. Environmental threats with the potential to erode the habitability of the planet from beneath us are forcing humanity to consider national security in far broader terms than that guaranteed solely by force of arms.

Military means are not only impotent in the face of environmental security threats but are an obstacle to their resolution. Weapons production can directly cause environmental damage. And the military consumes much of the resources needed to stem environmental degradation. Reversing the arms race, however, poses a daunting challenge to the ingenuity and collaborative spirit of diplomats and grassroots activists alike. Because environmental security requires cooperative solutions, though, replacing adversarial military alliances with global environmental coalitions could lay the foundation for a more cooperative and secure world.

Not only has it become increasingly evident that a militaristic definition of national security is outmoded, we are now witnessing an

> "Environmental threats with the potential to erode the habitability of the planet are forcing humanity to consider national security in far broader terms than that guaranteed solely by force of arms."

era in which the system of monolithic opposing blocs dominated by superpowers is evolving into a multipolar and more economically interdependent world. A new "geo-economics" has come to rival geopolitics as the central political dynamic. Most world leaders nonetheless continue to accept the traditional definition of security based on military might. Yet the well-being of nations *and* their individual citizens depends as well on economic vitality, social justice, and ecological stability. Pursuing military security at the cost of these other factors is akin to dismantling a house to salvage materials to erect a fence around it.

Now, as the cold war is starting to wind down, the debate about the essence of national security is broadening. Several factors are coalescing in a way that may make the nineties an unprecedented period for redirecting security policies. These include the "new thinking" in the Soviet Union that gave rise to *glasnost* (openness) and *perestroika* (restructuring), mounting budgetary constraints on military spending in many countries, renewed regard for the United Nations' role in conflict resolution and international cooperation, popular yearning for a less heavily armed world, and escalating international concern over the environment.

For the entire century, humanity has witnessed an unending arms race and an unprecedented toll of wars and destruction. With environmental degradation proceeding at a rate where it soon may become irreversible, security has come to embrace a new race—the race to save the planet.

A World at War

Over time, the ability to wage war has become increasingly more organized and institutionalized. Since World War II, war preparation—from standing armies to launch-on-warning—has become a permanent endeavor, often unrelated to any particular threat. The notion that countries should be able to defend themselves from any conceivable enemy at all times has found near-universal acceptance. As a result, the war-making institutions—the armed forces, the military bureaucracies, the intelligence agencies—have become fixtures, their operations lubricated by a permanent war economy that commands enormous economic and intellectual resources.[2]

The world has spent an estimated $17.5 trillion for military purposes since World War II (all monetary values in this paper are expressed in 1987 dollars). Annual expenditures are now approaching $1 trillion. (See Figure 1.) Adjusted for inflation, industrial countries have doubled their annual outlays since 1960. The Third World—with its ranks of independent states swelled by decolonization—increased expenditures more than sixfold. The developing countries' share of world military spending has thus risen from 6 percent of the total in 1965 to 18 percent by the mid-eighties.[3]

The world's armed forces are some 29 million strong, with an estimated 16 million additional persons employed in the world's arms industries. (See Table 1.) Paramilitary forces, which are not included in Table 1, probably number another 10 million. The International Labor Organization recently estimated total military-related employment worldwide (including national armed forces, militias, production workers, scientists, engineers, other technical professionals, and administrative personnel) at 60 to 80 million people, the higher range of which is roughly equivalent to the population of Mexico.[4]

The superpowers and their European allies are responsible for three-fourths of global military spending. But military aid, training programs, and the international arms trade—through which almost $800 billion worth of weapons has been transferred since 1960—have given many other countries access to increasingly sophisticated military technology. Added to long-standing fears of a spread of nuclear and chemical weapons is now a growing concern about the proliferation of ballistic missiles to deliver them.[5]

In addition to an enormous array of conventional arms held by nearly every country is an arsenal of about 50,000 nuclear warheads controlled by a relatively small number of states. Modern military

Figure 1: World Military Expenditures

technology has dramatically increased the destructive power of these weapons, the range and speed of their delivery vehicles, and the sophistication of targeting technologies. In less than 30 minutes, a single U.S. 10-warhead MX strategic missile or its Soviet counterpart can deliver a destructive force equivalent to more than 200 Hiroshima bombs to within 90 meters of a target 11,000 kilometers away.[6]

As Ruth Sivard writes in *World Military and Social Expenditures 1987–88*: "Every hamlet has been brought within the orbit of conflict, every inhabitant made a potential victim of random annihilation. Militarization presumably designed to insulate and protect the nation

Table 1: Armed Forces and Employment in Military Industries, Selected Countries, Early to Mid-eighties

Country	Workers[1]	Soldiers[2]	Country	Workers[1]	Soldiers[2]
	(thousands)			(thousands)	
Soviet Union	4,800	4,500	Spain	66	411
China	5,000	4,100	Indonesia	26	281
United States[3]	3,350	2,247	Israel	90	195
India[4]	280	1,515	Thailand	5	270
United Kingdom	700	335	South Africa	100	95
France	435	563	Argentina	60	129
Turkey	40	850	Philippines	5	157
North Korea	55	784	Peru	5	128
West Germany	290	495	Chile	3	124
Italy	160	531	Malaysia	3	124
Pakistan	40	644	Netherlands	18	103
South Korea	30	600	Sweden	28	69
Brazil	75	496	Singapore	11	59
Egypt	100	466	Austria	16	40
Taiwan	50	440	Norway	15	41
			TOTAL	15,814	20,834
			WORLD	n.a.	29,260

[1]Employed in arms-producing industries. Data for most countries listed, but particularly for China, must be treated as rough estimates.
[2]Military personnel employed by national defense ministries.
[3]There are an additional 1.1 million Department of Defense civil servants, bringing total U.S. defense-related employment to 6.7 million in 1988.
[4]An additional 30,000 persons work in military research and development.

Sources: U.S. Arms Control and Disarmament Agency, *World Military Expenditures and Arms Transfers 1987* (Washington, D.C.: U.S. Government Printing Office, 1988), for all data on armed forces. Arms production employment figures are compiled from: Peter Wilke and Herbert Wulf, "Manpower Conversion in Defense-related Industry," Disarmament and Employment Program, Working Paper No. 4 (Geneva: International Labor Organization, 1986); Michael Brzoska and Thomas Ohlson, "Trade in Major Conventional Weapons: The Changing Pattern," *Bulletin of Peace Proposals*, Vol. 17, No. 3-4, 1986; and other sources.

state has in fact united the world's population in a precarious mutual vulnerability." Arms ostensibly designed to enhance security now imperil humanity's very survival.[7]

Although arms races are more often a symptom of unresolved conflicts than the cause of them, they frequently gain a momentum of their own. Throughout history, governments have sought to develop and acquire more numerous and more effective arms—and the security, or the superiority and leverage over other nations, that possession of such arsenals seems to promise. But, ultimately, unilateral advantages prove short-lived. In the post-1945 superpower rivalry, for instance, the United States has sought security in technological superiority. With an uncompromising Soviet effort to match U.S. advances, however, innovations such as the intercontinental bomber, the multiple-warhead intercontinental missile, and the cruise missile resulted in only transitory advantages. Hence, each U.S. advance has ultimately rebounded into an imperative to advance an additional technological step. The result has been a rapid rate of obsolescence in military technology and a steadily changing and thus unstable relationship—in sum, greater mutual insecurity.

The prevailing doctrine of nuclear deterrence contributes to this instability. To be effective, deterrence requires a plausible threat. But threats are credible only if it appears that they can and will be carried out. Indeed, Zbigniew Brzezinski, President Jimmy Carter's national security adviser, argued that "a credible willingness to use [military power is necessary], and that implies its occasional use." Further, Caspar Weinberger, President Ronald Reagan's first secretary of defense, said that "U.S. contingency planning, to serve deterrence, must also envision the possible employment of nuclear weapons."[8]

The effort to make the threat of retaliation more credible explains why the arms race continues despite the already devastating forces in place. The scientific and technical communities are spurred to develop still more sophisticated, lethal, stealthy, and accurate weapons. In the process, both superpowers have moved beyond simple deterrence toward a war-fighting posture—designing ballistic missiles for first-strike missions, making missile silos more survivable against attack, and investigating the possibilities for anti-missile defense. *Discriminate Deterrence*, the 1988 report by the U.S. Commission on Integrated Long-term Strategy, assigns high priority to the pursuit of futuristic technologies and the capability for "discriminate nuclear strikes" to make war-fighting strategies a more "realistic" option.[9]

Possession of nuclear weapons by the United States and the Soviet Union spurred other nations, locked in intense rivalries with their neighbors, to seek their own nuclear arms. While none of them could hope to match the superpowers, these countries regard even a crude nuclear capability as insurance against defeat in a conventional battle. Once the Sino-Soviet relationship turned hostile, for instance, China worked feverishly to develop its own bomb. The success of that endeavor in 1964, however, in turn convinced India, which had lost a border war against the Chinese only two years earlier, that it needed to catch up with Beijing. And the supposedly "peaceful nuclear device" that New Delhi detonated a decade later set off alarm bells in Islamabad. Prime Minister Zulfikar Ali Bhutto vowed that his people would "eat grass," if necessary, in order to match their archrival, which had defeated Pakistan in 1971. Pakistan has not exploded a bomb, but it is now considered a de facto nuclear power. Additional regional rivalries and the special status that possession of a nuclear arsenal seems to confer have also stimulated the quest for the bomb in the Middle East, Latin America, and southern Africa.[10]

Clearly, worldwide military power is at unprecedented levels. Whether because of or despite this development, the number of wars and deaths has steadily increased. Some 22 wars have been fought in the eighties, more than in any previous decade in modern military history. Some 120 armed conflicts since 1945—most of them in the Third World—have killed at least 20 million people. Many of these conflicts have attracted little attention, but some are potential tinder-

> "Possession of nuclear weapons by the United States and Soviet Union spurred other nations, locked in intense rivalries with their neighbors, to seek their own nuclear arms."

boxes for global conflagration. It is without exaggeration that economist Kenneth Boulding has said that "national defense is now the greatest enemy of national security."[11]

At the same time that military might has escalated, aggression has become less successful. In the twentieth century, aggressors have won only 4 out of 10 wars; in the eighties, that ratio is down to 1 out of 10. Irrespective of the outcome of these wars, the prime losers have been civilians. Since World War I, the economic base and civilian population of an enemy have been regarded as acceptable targets in a "total war." Warfare is no longer limited to a delineated battlefield, blurring the distinction between combatants and civilians. Whether through direct casualties or war-induced starvation, civilians constitute a rapidly growing share of war victims: while they accounted for 52 percent of all deaths in the fifties, by the eighties their share had grown to 85 percent.[12]

Conventional wisdom holds that armed forces are maintained to guard against external enemies. In many Third World countries, however, the military has not been used to protect the interests of the population as a whole but instead those of a privileged class. As military takeovers in Chile, Guatemala, Indonesia, and Uganda in recent decades have demonstrated, the armed forces are an important instrument for preserving political and economic structures that deny basic needs and opportunities to the majority.[13]

It is not surprising, then, that by far the greatest number of armed conflicts (and approximately half of all war deaths) since World War II have been in the form of civil wars. Resort to military means may succeed in suppressing the expression of grievances, but it is unlikely to eliminate the roots of conflict. Strife arises from a host of ethnic, cultural, and political disputes and is often fueled by sharp socio-economic inequalities. In addition, the post-colonial era has seen the resurgence of centuries-old animosities that were aggravated by arbitrarily drawn boundaries or preferential treatment of certain population groups.[14]

When Third World governments do engage in warfare against another state, the combat is usually of short duration because their staying power is severely circumscribed by limited financial resources, weak civic institutions, and a lack of legitimacy of the warring regime. Wars of attrition risk major political and economic breakdown. As Mohammed Ayoob of the National University of Singapore explained: "These constraints soon outweigh the perceived political or military benefits for which the wars were launched." Exceptions occur when outside powers stoke the fires or, as in the Iran-Iraq war, when large oil revenues footed the bill.[15]

One reason why military means are still at the center of security thinking is that military prowess has not lost its usefulness in the eyes of those who wield it. By using force, or threatening to, national leaders still hope to coerce other countries—to influence their economic policies and political systems. Weaker nations, in turn, feel they have little choice but to try to keep up lest they become vulnerable to stronger neighbors. Governments frequently comprehend military prowess as the ultimate expression—and protector—of national sovereignty. Legitimate and illegitimate uses of military power are often so tightly interwoven that it becomes difficult to distinguish between strictly defensive policies and unbridled power politics.

Whether rich or poor, militarily strong or weak, countries still lack a reliable international framework on which to depend for security. Robert Johansen, director of the Institute for International Peace Studies at Notre Dame University, pointed out that "the very nature of the system of sovereign states encourages armed rivalry between governments. Because the system provides no impartial, dependable way to prevent one government from violently coercing another, governments seek arms as a means of self-help."[16]

The Drain of a Permanent War Economy

Even in the absence of armed conflict, preoccupation with building military power can sap the economic vitality of nations. In his

> "Both superpowers have spent enough on their armed forces to undermine their infrastructure, retard civilian R&D, and diminish economic competitiveness."

celebrated work *The Rise and Fall of the Great Powers*, British historian Paul Kennedy chronicles what he calls the dangers of "imperial overstretch"—the impact of heavy military commitments on economic vitality. One cannot drink rocket fuel, commute in a tank, or live in a missile silo. Neither do such military goods enhance an economy's capacity to increase the standard of living. In the long run, the resource drain a large military sector imposes on an economy can cripple its ability to function effectively.[17]

On average, the world's nations spend some 6 percent of their gross national product (GNP) on defense, but that average conceals tremendous differences between individual countries. (See Table 2.) While many economists consider such a share too small to elicit much concern, there is in fact reason for worry. For one, during 1980–85, the growth in global military outlays outpaced that of world economic output for the first time since 1960, meaning that a larger portion of wealth went to the military. (See Table 3.) Moreover, GNP is a poor yardstick for measuring the impact of military spending on the civilian economy. A statistical aggregate of monetary values, this indicator tells little about the productive capacities of an economy and nothing about how they are being used. The military sector saps the civilian economy far beyond the effect suggested by a simple comparison with GNP.[18]

Among industrialized countries, the detrimental effects of maintaining a permanent war economy are most pronounced in the Soviet Union and the United States. Both superpowers have spent enough on their armed forces to undermine their infrastructure, retard civilian research and development, and diminish economic competitiveness. Recognizing these concerns, Soviet President Mikhail Gorbachev has stated that reversing the arms race with the United States is a prerequisite for invigorating his country's ailing economy. The Soviet Union's chronic shortages of consumer goods and their low quality have become legendary, and *glasnost* has revealed that inflation and budget deficits are serious national problems.[19]

Civilian R&D and capital and consumer goods production in the Soviet Union have suffered as military projects were assigned top

Table 2: Military Share of Gross National Product, Selected Countries, 1985

Country	Share
	(percent)
Iraq*	42.5
Israel*	25.8
Saudi Arabia	24.4
Syria	22.8
North Korea	22.2
Libya*	17.8
Nicaragua	16.8
Egypt	14.2
Soviet Union	12.5
Ethiopia	9.1
Afghanistan*	7.7
Taiwan	7.6
Mozambique	7.4
Iran*	7.2
China	6.7
United States	6.6
East Germany	6.4
South Korea	5.5
United Kingdom*	5.3
South Africa*	4.2
France	4.1
India	3.8
West Germany	3.2
Japan	1.0
Brazil	1.0
WORLD AVERAGE	6.1

*Indicates 1984 data.

Source: U.S. Arms Control and Disarmament Agency, *World Military Expenditures and Arms Transfers 1987* (Washington, D.C.: Government Printing Office, 1988).

Table 3: Real Annual Growth of Economic Output and Military Expenditures, 1960–85[1]

Region	1960–70	1970–80	1980–85	1960–85
	(percent)			
Western Industrial Countries				
Gross National Product	4.9	3.1	2.2	3.6
Military Spending	2.9	–0.8	5.7	2.0
Third World[2]				
Gross National Product	7.6	6.2	3.1	6.1
Military Spending	11.7	2.7	2.1	6.1
Centrally Planned Economies[3]				
Gross National Product	4.4	3.3	1.7	3.4
Military Spending	3.2	3.9	1.3	3.1
World Average				
Gross National Product	5.0	3.5	2.2	3.9
Military Spending	4.1	1.6	3.2	2.9

[1]Military spending figures start with 1961; all annual growth rates calculated from data expressed in constant dollars.
[2]Includes China.
[3]Estimates for centrally planned economies are likely to have a wide margin of error.

Sources: Worldwatch Institute, based on U.S. Central Intelligence Agency, *Handbook of Economic Statistics 1987* (Springfield, Va.: National Technical Information Service, 1987), and U.S. Arms Control and Disarmament Agency, *World Military Expenditures and Arms Transfers* (Washington, D.C.: U.S. Government Printing Office, various editions).

priority in both quality and quantity of resources. Stanley Cohn, professor of economics at the State University of New York, estimated that the military's share of durable goods consumption rose sharply during the sixties and seventies, from 19 percent in 1965 to 30 percent in 1980. Though more recent data are not available, the trend has likely continued.[20]

Even though the military's share of total durable goods consumption in the United States is considerably lower, it has almost doubled from 6 percent in the seventies to just under 11 percent in the early eighties. In some industries, the proportion of output that goes to the military is substantially higher. (See Table 4.)[21]

In the late fifties, the Soviet Union was on the verge of becoming an efficient mass producer of machine tools, with the prospect of assuming a world leadership role, according to Seymour Melman, professor emeritus of industrial engineering at Columbia University. That promise never materialized, however, because the money and talent to develop a competitive industry were redirected to a massive military space program. Today, the Soviets find they are unable to compete in world industrial markets, having been passed even by newly industrialized countries such as South Korea.[22]

The most critical negative repercussion of military spending on the economy is in the area of research and development. The research intensity of military products has been estimated to be as high as 20 times that of civilian products. A prolonged, heavy emphasis on defense-related R&D impairs a country's innovative capacity by drawing scientific talent away from the civilian sector. A large pool of a nation's talents is then unavailable to keep industry competitive, or to address social and environmental needs.[23]

World military R&D has grown from $13 billion a year in 1960 to an estimated $80 to $100 billion in 1986, an amount that exceeds the combined governmental research outlays on developing new energy technologies, improving human health, raising agricultural productivity, and controlling pollution. The two superpowers are responsible for approximately 85 percent of this total, and China, France, the United Kingdom, and West Germany collectively for another 10 percent. Military research accounts for at least one-fourth of all R&D funds and for a comparable portion of all the scientists and engineers engaged in research. According to Gregory Bischak, a senior economist at Employment Research Associates (ERA) in Lansing, Michigan, an estimated 27 percent of all U.S. scientists

Table 4: Military Consumption of U.S. Industrial Output in Selected Industries, 1977 and 1985

Industry	1977	1985
	(percent)	
Shipbuilding	45	93
Aircraft	43	66
Radio and TV Communications	35	50
Machine Tools/Cutting	3	34
Engineering Instruments	19	28
Optical Instruments	14	24
Electronic Components	15	20
Machine Tools/Forming	2	15
Ball Bearings	7	15
Steel Mills	5	12
Copper Mining	5	11

Source: David K. Henry and Richard P. Oliver, "The Defense Buildup, 1977–1985: Effects on Production and Employment," *Monthly Labor Review* (Washington, D.C.: U.S. Department of Labor), August 1987.

and engineers are engaged in military-related work; in the United Kingdom, that figure is probably over 30 percent.[24]

The share of public R&D outlays that goes to the military is as high as 70 percent in the United States and an estimated 60 percent in the Soviet Union. On the other hand, some countries have benefited economically by holding that portion down. It is as low as 4 percent in Japan, and below 1 percent in Denmark and Belgium. (See Figure 2.) When private R&D funds are taken into consideration, the military share drops but the discrepancy in priorities between different countries remains. In the United States, combined military-related R&D expenditures in the mid-eighties may have been equivalent to as much as 45 percent of total government and private spending,

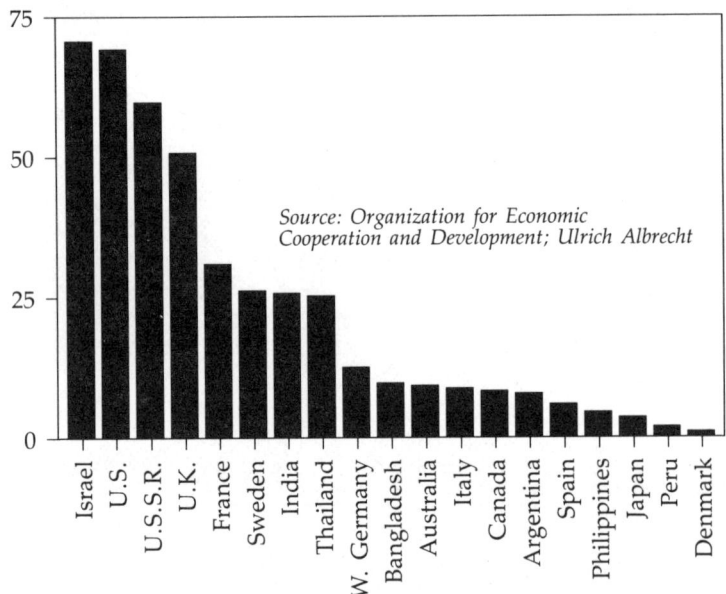

Figure 2: **Expenditures for Military Research & Development, Mid-eighties**

according to the Council on Economic Priorities in New York. Similarly, the United Kingdom devotes close to 30 percent to military research, France 20 percent, but West Germany only 5 percent and Japan less than 1 percent.[25]

Proponents of large-scale military spending contend that while resources are diverted from the civilian economy, scientific break-

> "The U.S. Air Force's sponsorship of computer-controlled machine tools in the fifties resulted in an overly complex technology that failed to keep American industry competitive."

throughs from defense-related research—"spinoffs"—more than offset that disadvantage. It is true that military sponsorship played an important role in the development of technologies like nuclear power, aerospace, computers, and semiconductors. But relative to the lavish resources devoted to military R&D, the spinoffs have been meager because the results of applied research, which constitutes the bulk of military research (some 90 percent in both the United States and the United Kingdom in 1985), are less transferable than those of basic research. Fewer than 1 percent of patents resulting from U.S. Navy–sponsored R&D are commercially licensed, for example, compared with 13 percent of Department of Agriculture patents.[26]

Many military-developed technologies that found civilian applications had to undergo significant redesign before they were commercially practical. Because victory through superior technology is an overriding goal in the military realm, product specifications are geared to maximum performance, with little attention devoted to cost. This is the opposite approach to that in the development of civilian products, where durability and low cost, not the extreme demands of combat conditions, are key. Hans-Peter Dürr, director of the Werner Heisenberg Institute of Physics in Munich, West Germany, has asked with respect to the civilian application of technologies under development for missile defense (the Strategic Defense Initiative): "The ability to forge a sword may be useful for making plowshares—but do we need the ability to burn holes in metal at a range of 1,800 miles?"[27]

To the extent that spinoffs are achieved, they could be accomplished more directly and at considerably lower cost through civilian scientific research. A study by David Noble of Drexel University in Philadelphia, for example, demonstrates that the U.S. Air Force's sponsorship of computer-controlled machine tools in the fifties resulted in an overly complex and expensive technology that failed to keep American industry competitive with Japan and West Germany in later decades. By 1978, the United States had become a net importer of machine tools; by 1983, Japanese firms accounted for over half of all computer-controlled machining centers sold in the United States, up from only 4 percent in 1974.[28]

The real question therefore concerns the benefits foregone by giving the military priority in R&D allocations. Simon Ramo, a cofounder of TRW Inc., one of the leading U.S. military contractors, admitted in 1980 that "in the past thirty years, had the total dollars we spent on military R&D been expended instead in those areas of science and technology promising the most economic progress, we probably would be today where we are going to find ourselves arriving in the year 2000."[29]

The military has also assumed a prominent profile in capital investment. A United Nations expert group estimated that world military expenditures in 1981 were equal to one-fourth of all annual fixed investments (durable industrial equipment and structures). In the United States, that share is considerably higher. According to Lloyd Dumas, professor of political economy at the University of Texas, the Pentagon's share of net investment in plant and equipment undertaken by all U.S. manufacturers in 1982 (including the 20,000 prime military contractors and over 100,000 subcontractors) came to nearly 38 percent. The physical capital (industrial equipment, buildings, land holdings) owned by the U.S. military in 1983—valued conservatively at $475 billion—was equivalent to almost half that owned by all U.S. manufacturers combined.[30]

A comparison of selected member countries of the Organization for Economic Cooperation and Development—the non-communist industrialized countries, abbreviated as OECD—suggests an inverse relationship between the share of gross domestic product spent on the military, and investment, economic growth, and productivity trends. Similarly, an econometric model developed by ERA shows that the U.S. military buildup in 1981–85 "generated $39 billion less investment activity . . . than normal civilian spending would have."[31]

While the military has enjoyed a cornucopia, civilian infrastructure has been starved of funds. The amount of capital devoted by the

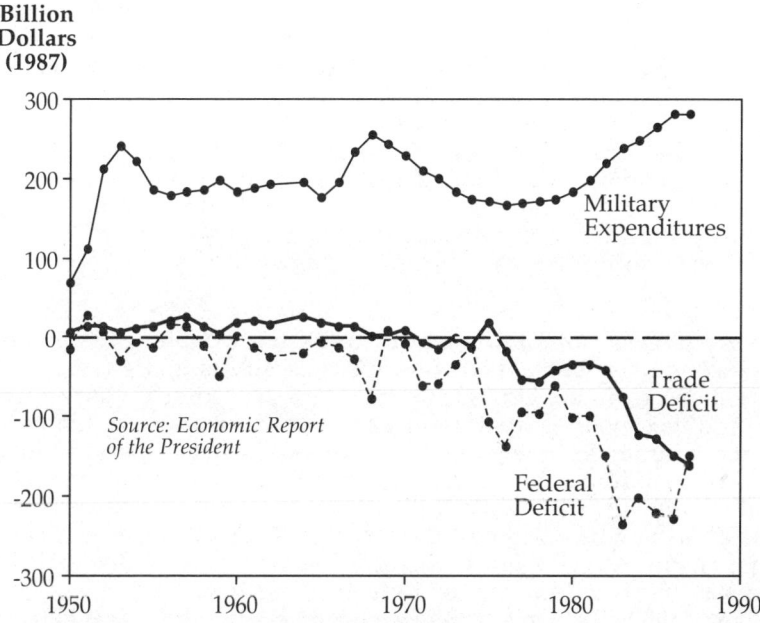

Figure 3: U.S. Military Expenditures and Economic Deficits

United States to building military power ($9.2 trillion between 1948 and 1988) exceeds the cumulative monetary value of all human-made wealth in the United States. An estimated two-thirds of that wealth— which statisticians refer to as civilian "fixed reproducible tangible wealth," and which includes items such as industrial plants and machinery, communications and transport systems, buildings, bridges, and water and sewage systems—is now in dire need of reconstruction.[32]

A 1988 study by ERA's Michael Dee Oden confirmed earlier assessments that military outlays generate less employment per dollar than do civilian expenditures. The net increase in U.S. military spending between 1981 and 1985—some $190 billion—created an estimated 7.2 million job-years of work over that period; had the equivalent sum been spent on civilian activities, it would have generated 8.4 million job-years. In the United States, according to Oden, there is also strong evidence that large-scale military spending "accelerates inflation in periods of full employment and limits the fall in the inflation rate in deflationary periods." A report commissioned by the United Nations provides evidence that this effect occurs in other Western industrialized countries as well.[33]

Military largess cannot be blamed for all the troubles of contemporary economies, but it has contributed a substantial share. In the current decade in the United States, record peacetime military spending and tax policies that reduced federal revenues combined to trigger a dramatic rise in federal budget deficits. Years of heavy military spending have also contributed to a deterioration in civilian productivity growth, which in turn has undermined the ability of U.S. industry to remain cost competitive. Compounded by a strong dollar in the early eighties, this has led to a loss of domestic and overseas markets, and hence to a growing trade gap. (See Figure 3.) Until 1982, the United States never registered a trade deficit in manufactured goods. Even in high-technology trade—a traditional forte—the United States moved from a $27 billion surplus to a $2.6 billion deficit between 1980 and 1986. Ironically, industries heavily engaged in military contracting, such as aircraft, electronics, and machine tools, have suffered some of the most pronounced losses of market share.[34]

Both the United States and the Soviet Union have pursued an elusive military superiority at the cost of their international economic standing. Thus, if either side claims to have won the cold war, it is surely a pyrrhic victory. As they have fought to an apparent standstill, Japan has emerged from the ruins of World War II to become the fastest growing industrial economy and the country with the largest trade surplus—the real winner of the superpower arms race.[35]

Armaments and Underdevelopment

Although the military expenditures of most Third World countries are minute compared with those of the superpowers—either one of which spends more than all the developing countries combined—they nonetheless entail a heavy economic burden on individual nations. The available data are too limited to make empirical proof conclusive, but it appears that, just as in the industrial countries, military expenditures are more likely to hinder than to promote economic growth and development in the Third World.

Relatively few developing countries produce major weapons domestically, and collectively they account for only a small portion of the roughly $200 billion worth of annual world military production. Among the 26 Third World arms producers, India and Israel together have accounted for over half of the Third World's production of major arms between 1950 and 1984. (For the sake of simplicity, some nations with fairly advanced industrial and technological capabilities have been included in the Third World category in this analysis.) Brazil, though a relative newcomer to the arms-manufacturing community, is fast catching up and has become the Third World's leading exporter. (See Table 5).[36]

Establishing an arms industry has been justified as a shortcut to industrialization—an attempt made in Latin America as early as the thirties. The policy of stimulating civilian industry through arms production, however, has largely been a failure. According to Nicole Ball of the National Security Archive, a private research organization in Washington, D.C., the experience of Argentina, Brazil, Egypt, Indonesia, South Africa, and South Korea suggests that "no Third World country can hope to support arms production of any magnitude if it does not *already* possess a reasonably strong, diversified industrial sector." [Emphasis added.] In fact, Brazilian analyst Clóvis Brigagão has claimed that in Brasilia "it was assumed from the start that [the development of a domestic] defense industry would be accomplished at whatever cost to the rest of the economy."[37]

Table 5: Third World Producers of Major Weapons, 1950–84[1]

Country	(percent)	Country	(percent)
India	31	Argentina	5
Israel	23	South Korea	4
South Africa	9	Egypt	2
Brazil	9	ASEAN Countries[2]	2
Taiwan	8	Others	1
North Korea	6		

[1]In percent of total Third World production.
[2]Indonesia, Malaysia, Philippines, Singapore, Thailand.

Source: Michael Brzoska and Thomas Ohlson, *Arms Production in the Third World* (SIPRI, 1986).

In order to finance its crushing foreign debt (an estimated 12 to 20 percent of which was contributed by the military sector), Brazil has become an arms peddler willing to sell abroad to almost any customer. Moreover, the Brazilian military sector has not so much become the engine of industrial development as a refuge for civilian enterprises hurt by Brasilia's policies in response to the debt crisis. Favored by the government because it can bring in foreign exchange, the country's military industry has not had to cope with the kind of economic constraints that most civilian industries must face.[38]

Israel has perhaps the most thoroughly militarized economy. Very high proportions of GNP (an average of 22 percent between 1979 and 1986), government budget (40 percent in 1985), R&D spending (71 percent of public *and* private expenditures in 1986), and the labor force (28 percent in 1985) are tied up in the military sector. Particularly in the area of capital goods production, the Israeli arms industry is the dominant sector of the economy; by one estimate, the military sector accounts for 30–40 percent of industrial production.[39]

But according to Israeli economist Simcha Bahiri, the military has been no boon to the country's development. He concludes that "the most rapid period of Israel's development occurred when the defense/GNP ratio was at its lowest." In the seventies and eighties, military spending has become a heavy economic burden. As the country's economy has become progressively militarized, it has grown weaker—characterized by rampant inflation, large external debts, trade deficits, and falling non-military exports. In 1984, more than 40 percent of Israel's foreign debt could be attributed to military loans.[40]

Most Third World countries do not have any significant domestic arms production capacity. By far the largest portion of their military budgets goes to pay for personnel and operating costs rather than to finance weapons procurement and military construction projects. Hence, for these countries, the impact of the military sector is primarily in the form of salaries and military-related skills. To the extent that they are spent on indigenous products and services, military salaries stimulate the domestic economy. However, there is no special economic bonus that could not have been derived from civilian expenditures instead.[41]

Military training could expand the pool of skilled workers where it does not compete with the civilian sector for the most qualified individuals. Because of the generally higher pay scales in the defense area in many countries, however, there is often a significant drain of skilled workers to the military sector. Moreover, armed forces training is frequently highly military-specific and therefore not easily transferable to the civilian sector. Where they do find application, military-derived skills are likely to be oriented toward capital-intensive, labor-saving techniques in countries where labor is abundant and either unemployment or underemployment is the problem.[42]

Thus, rather than being a stimulus to economic development, the armed forces of many countries are feeding on their civilian economies. The Indonesian officer corps has taken over ownership and management of the most dynamic industrial sectors, from which the armed forces derive additional revenues equal to 20–35 percent of the official military budget. In Thailand and Guatemala, the military is a large landowner. The Egyptian military has become the single largest agro-industrial organization, producing 18 percent of domestic food in 1985–86. In Turkey, the military controls plants that produce automobiles and petrochemicals.[43]

When improving people's living standards requires all available resources for productive investment, every dollar, rupee, peso, or naira spent for the military is money foregone for human development. "The failures of the present security system are as serious for many persons living at peace as for those suffering war," noted Robert Johansen of the Institute for International Peace Studies. This assessment is borne out by the pervasiveness of unmet human needs: some 770 million persons are malnourished and 14 million children die of hunger-related causes each year; 100 million individuals live without adequate shelter; 880 million adults are unable to read and write; and some 1.3 billion persons lack access to safe drinking water. President Dwight D. Eisenhower put it eloquently 36 years ago: "Every gun that is made, every warship launched, every rocket fired represents, in the final analysis, a theft from those who hunger and are not fed, who are cold and are not clothed."[44]

Despite the immensity of unmet social needs, many countries nevertheless accord the military priority in their budgets. World Bank data for a sample of 36 developing countries show that 20 of them increased their military expenditures as a percentage of their GNP during the 1972–86 period. All but 3 of them—the Philippines, Singapore, and South Korea—simultaneously reduced the portion of outlays going to either health and education or both. India, not included in this sample, cut social programs for the poor while tripling military expenditures between 1980 and 1988.[45]

Loans acquired for the purchase of military equipment have strongly contributed to Third World indebtedness. Unproductive in nature, these credits failed to generate the foreign exchange necessary for

> "Loans acquired for the purchase of military equipment have strongly contributed to Third World indebtedness."

their repayment. During the fifties and sixties, this did not seem of much concern because most arms deliveries to developing countries were either outright gifts or provided under very favorable credit terms. But since the early seventies, arms transfers have increasingly taken the form of commercial sales, directly competing with civilian imports.[46]

Had non-oil-exporting developing countries made no foreign arms purchases during 1972–82, their accumulated debts by the end of that period would have been perhaps 20–25 percent smaller. Lloyd Dumas of the University of Texas has pointed out that "if the Third World's *share* of world military spending had been the same in those years as it was in the early sixties, the less developed nations as a group would have saved enough money from this one source to finance repayment of nearly two-thirds of their outstanding debt."[47]

The final irony of the failure of militarization to spur industrialization is that, to the extent that military expenditures have contributed to indebtedness, they have actually undermined national security. Indebtedness has made many countries susceptible to creditor pressures and given the International Monetary Fund a powerful voice in national decision-making, thus sharply compromising sovereignty. In addition, the austerity programs imposed on these countries have deprived uncounted millions of people of the most fundamental elements of social and economic security. Riots—in response to cuts in food subsidies and social programs—have shaken the major cities of a growing number of countries, including most recently Algeria and Venezuela.[48]

Environment and Security

Countries are prepared to make considerable sacrifices in order to defend their national sovereignty and territory against foreign invaders. So far, however, they are not showing an equal determination to guard against environmental threats, whether they be a clear and present danger or a future one. Yet environmental degradation imperils nations' most fundamental aspect of security by undermining the natural support systems on which all of human activity depends.

According to the United Nations Environment Program (UNEP), 35 percent of the earth's land surface—on which about one-fifth of the world's population depends for its livelihood—is threatened by desertification, a principal threat to the economic well-being of many countries. But in nations such as Ethiopia, India, and Mauritania, which are severely affected by desertification, it is human survival itself that is at stake. Plowing highly erodible land, drawing down water tables through overpumping for irrigation, salinization of irrigated land, overgrazing of rangelands, and deforestation are the principal causes of desertification. In many countries, these practices are the result of social and economic inequities. Population growth, unequal land distribution, and the lack of secure land tenure are forcing landless peasants onto marginal lands that are less fertile and highly erodible or, coaxed by national resettlement programs and the lure of hidden treasures, into cutting down tropical forests to create new cropland or rangeland, even though that land will sustain agriculture only for a few years.[49]

Particularly on the African continent, desertification has sapped the food-growing potential to the point where the livelihood of rural peoples is in acute jeopardy. During the eighties, the increase in food output has fallen behind population growth in dozens of developing countries. "Food insecure" people—those who do not have enough food for normal health and physical activity—number more than 100 million in Africa alone, according to the World Bank. In countries where agriculture still forms the backbone of the national economy, these trends, unless reversed, portend severe economic dislocation and social disintegration, as the inability of countries to feed their own populations increases and rural people are forced to earn a living in cities already characterized by massive unemployment or underemployment.[50]

Reliance on food imports compromises a nation's sovereignty in ways that are unaffected by even the strongest of armed forces.

> "Because environmental degradation and pollution respect no human-drawn borders, they jeopardize not only the security of the country in which they occur, but also that of others near and far."

Moreover, the need to import large and growing amounts of food exacts a heavy toll on a country's trade balance, particularly when grain prices and external debt are rising. Yet despite these dangers, few countries have been able to take adequate measures to safeguard the long-term productivity of their lands. For example, to date only one—the United States—has in place a program to take highly erodible cropland out of production and to convert it to less-intensive, sustainable uses.[51]

Because environmental degradation and pollution respect no human-drawn borders, they jeopardize not only the security of the country in which they occur, but also that of others, near and far. Most often, this transboundary effect is simply the inevitable consequence of meteorological and hydrological conditions and other natural cycles. But occasionally, governments and private companies take active measures to export pollution—building smokestacks tall enough to disperse airborne pollutants beyond their borders, for example, or exporting undesired wastes. The growing garbage crisis in industrial countries has spawned an international waste trade of largely unknown proportions, with shipments going to nations hoping to derive foreign exchange, many of which cannot adequately monitor them to prevent illegal and hazardous dumping.[52]

Border-transcending environmental degradation most immediately affects neighboring countries. Because they form a natural barrier, rivers play an important role in territorial demarcation. As a consequence, however, watersheds frequently fall under the jurisdiction of several hostile states. An estimated 40 percent of the world's population depends for drinking water, irrigation, or hydropower on the 214 major river systems shared by two or more countries; 12 of these waterways are shared by five or more nations.[53]

Disputes over water use and quality simmer in virtually all parts of the world. (See Table 6.) These involve reduced water flow (and increased evaporation) through dams constructed by upstream riparian countries, water diversion, industrial and agrochemical pollution, salinization of streams through heavy irrigation, siltation of rivers,

Table 6: Unresolved International Water Issues, Mid-eighties

Rivers	Countries Involved in Dispute	Subject of Dispute
Nile	Egypt, Ethiopia, Sudan	Siltation, flooding, water flow/diversion
Euphrates, Tigris	Iraq, Syria, Turkey	Reduced water flow, salinization (constraints on irrigation & hydropower)
Jordan, Yarmuk, Litani, West Bank aquifer	Israel, Jordan, Syria, Lebanon	Water flow/diversion
Indus, Sutlei	India, Pakistan	Irrigation
Brahmaputra, Ganges	Bangladesh, India	Siltation, flooding, water flow
Salween/Nu Jiang	Burma, China	Siltation, flooding
Mekong	Kampuchea, Laos, Thailand, Vietnam	Water flow, flooding
Paraná	Argentina, Brazil	Dam, land inundation
Lauca	Bolivia, Chile	Dam, salinization
Rio Grande, Colorado	Mexico, United States	Salinization, water flow, agrochemical pollution
Great Lakes	Canada, United States	Water diversion
Rhine	France, Netherlands, Switzerland, West Germany	Industrial pollution
Maas, Schelde	Belgium, Netherlands	Salinization, industrial pollution
Elbe	Czechoslovakia, East and West Germany	Industrial pollution
Werra/Weser	East Germany, West Germany	Industrial pollution
Szamos	Hungary, Romania	Industrial pollution

Sources: "Environment and Conflict," Earthscan Briefing Document 40 (International Institute for Environment and Development: London, 1984); Norman Myers, *Not Far Afield: U.S. Interests and the Global Environment* (Washington, D.C.: World Resources Institute, 1988); Joyce R. Starr and Daniel C. Stoll (eds.), *The Politics of Scarcity: Water in the Middle East* (Boulder and London: Westview Press, 1988); P.C. Mayer-Tasch, *Die Verseuchte Landkarte* (Munich, West Germany: C.H. Beck, 1987); K. Bouwer, "Geographische Aspekte Grenzüberschreitender Umweltprobleme" in Kurt Tudyka (ed.), *Umweltpolitik in Ost- und Westeuropa* (Opladen: Leske & Budrich, 1988); "Where Dams Can Cause Wars," *Economist*, July 18, 1987; and other sources.

and floods aggravated by deforestation and soil erosion. On the Rhine watershed in Europe, for example, some 20 million downstream users, particularly in the Netherlands, must have their drinking water filtered for heavy metals, hazardous chemicals, and salt deposited further upstream in France, Switzerland, and West Germany. An accident at the Sandoz Inc. chemical facilities near Basel, Switzerland, in 1986, which heavily polluted the river with fungicides and mercury, highlights the interdependence of the riparian countries and the potential for recriminations among them.[54]

Control over the Nile waters is a matter that casts a shadow over relations among Egypt, the Sudan, and Ethiopia. Egypt is already using more water than it was allotted under a 1959 pact with Sudan; irrigation plans for the nineties reveal that Egypt's needs could surpass its allocated water share by as much as one-fifth. Upstream, it seems that only a lack of funds is preventing Ethiopia from making good on its plan to divert more water from the Blue Nile tributary, which would directly affect Egypt's water supplies. Egyptian Foreign Minister Butros Ghali warned in early 1985 that "the next war in our region will be over the waters of the Nile, not politics."[55]

Deforestation seems an unlikely source of tension between nations. Yet by aggravating soil erosion and silt accumulation in riverbeds, it can lead to devastating floods. Denuded watersheds in the Ethiopian highlands have exacerbated floods in neighboring Sudan, devastating its capital, Khartoum, in 1988. The frequency and magnitude of flooding in Bangladesh has markedly increased, partly due to deforestation in the Himalayas since mid-century. The flood in 1988 left 25 million persons homeless—a threat to national security on par with most wars. And in India, flood-prone areas have doubled to 40 million hectares between 1970 and 1980. This problem can be effectively counteracted only if Bangladesh, Bhutan, China, India, and Nepal all agree to cooperate in forestry management and waterflow regulation. To that end, Bangladesh is advocating the establishment of a regional water authority. China has expressed willingness to cooperate at least on a bilateral basis, but India so far remains opposed to a multilateral solution.[56]

The impact of pollution originating in one country is no longer felt solely in adjacent or proximate countries, as transboundary air pollution strikingly illustrates. Toxic clouds carrying hazardous substances can traverse the entire globe before dispersing or falling to earth. Insecticides from Asia and southern Europe, for instance, are found in Arctic and Antarctic waters. The most notorious example of transboundary air pollution is acid precipitation. The result of nitrogen and sulfur oxides, acid rain is taking a terrible toll on aquatic life and forests. It has led to a war of words between the United States and Canada, which receives more than 50 percent of its acid deposition from its southern neighbor. All European countries are involved in an intensive exchange of air pollutants, but Norway and Sweden are involuntary *net* importers of sulfur dioxide, originating primarily in the United Kingdom. Norway's foreign minister considers the British reluctance to address the issue a problem as serious for mutual relations as trade and defense. (See Table 7.)[57]

The powerful explosion at the nuclear reactor in Chernobyl in 1986 hurled radioactive debris far into the atmosphere, transporting it across large areas of the planet's northern hemisphere. The recriminations against the Soviet Union for failing to provide an adequate and timely warning of the accident soon led to broader concerns about the siting of nuclear reactors, enrichment and reprocessing facilities, and radioactive-waste dumps. In Europe, 119 nuclear power plants are located within 100 kilometers of a national border. The Danish parliament decided to ask Sweden to close a plant 30 kilometers from Copenhagen. The French government rejected a similar plea by local West German authorities in the Saarland to cancel construction of four reactors at Cattenom. Similar issues have produced strains between Ireland and the United Kingdom, Austria and both West Germany and Czechoslovakia, Hong Kong and China, and Argentina and Chile.[58]

Spurred by a stream of new scientific evidence, attention is now shifting to those aspects of environmental degradation that have

Table 7: Imports and Exports of Sulfur Dioxide Emissions, 1984

	Total Emissions[1]	Total Deposition[2]	Share of Emissions Exported	Share of Deposition Imported
	(million metric tons of SO_2)		(percent)	
Norway	0.2	0.6	57	90
Sweden	0.5	1.2	57	83
Czechoslovakia	3.6	3.3	62	59
Poland	4.0	3.5	60	54
France	2.9	2.6	57	54
West Germany	3.7	2.6	67	53
East Germany	4.2	1.8	72	36
Soviet Union[3]	19.9	16.1	47	35
Italy	3.2	2.1	56	32
Spain	2.3	1.7	46	28
United Kingdom	4.5	2.1	64	20

[1]From domestic sources.
[2]From domestic and foreign sources.
[3]European part only.

Source: Tomasz Zylicz, "European Airborne Pollution: Economic, Social and Political Aspects of a Possible Reduction Program," Warsaw University, unpublished manuscript, 1986, based on data from the Economic Commission for Europe, Cooperative Program for the Monitoring and Evaluation of the Long-range Transmission of Air Pollution in Europe.

an all-encompassing, global effect from which no nation can insulate itself. Even though their full impact may be felt only years or decades from today, the depletion of the ozone layer and the global warming trend can no longer be considered to be hypothetical threats; their effect can only be countered if policies that drastically reduce the reliance on fossil fuels and ozone destroying chemicals are adopted quickly.

The ozone layer in the stratosphere, which protects life on earth from harmful ultraviolet radiation, has begun to thin globally. The extent of its depletion varies seasonally and according to latitude, but a 1988 study by the U.S. National Air and Space Administration showed that the global average concentration declined by about 2 percent between 1969 and 1986. Failure to rapidly phase out the chlorofluorocarbons (CFCs) and other substances that decay into ozone depleting chemicals presents a grave threat to human health (through increased skin cancer rates and weakened human immune systems), to agricultural productivity, and to marine fisheries everywhere on earth.[59]

The security of nations is similarly compromised by the greenhouse effect—the specter of global climate change brought on by the accumulation of carbon dioxide and other gases in the atmosphere that trap heat. Global average temperature records from 1880 to the present reveal a gradual warming trend compatible with greenhouse scenarios predicted by computer simulations. The prospect of an accelerated warming of the earth in coming decades—now widely accepted as a realistic possibility—puts the conditions essential to the stability of the biosphere in jeopardy. Shifting precipitation patterns and vegetation zones and rising sea levels caused by global warming threaten to disrupt a wide range of human and natural systems. The greenhouse effect could disrupt crop harvests, inundate heavily populated low-lying coastal areas like the Bengal and Nile deltas, upset human settlement patterns, and undermine biological diversity.[60]

In an impassioned speech before the United Nations General Assembly in October 1987, Maumoon Abdul Gayoom, president of the Maldives, declared that a sea-level rise of only one meter would jeopardize the survival of his 1,196-island nation. He observed that "we did not contribute to the impending catastrophe to our nation and alone we cannot save ourselves." His comments highlight the particular predicament that Third World nations face. Except for China (which burns large amounts of coal) and Brazil (where the decimation of the Amazon rain forest causes large-scale carbon re-

> "Spurred by new scientific evidence, attention is now shifting to those aspects of environmental degradation that have a global effect, from which no nation can insulate itself."

lease), global warming and ozone depletion are caused primarily by industrial countries: they account for 69 percent of carbon dioxide emissions and 84 percent of CFC production. Thus, as Third World commentators point out, while only a handful of countries enjoy most of the economic benefits associated with the use of fossil fuels and CFCs (the latter are used primarily as aerosol propellants, foam-blowing agents, industrial solvents, and refrigerants), all of humanity will suffer from the ecological repercussions. In fact, densely populated Asian countries, where rice is produced on floodplains, would suffer the most from rising sea levels, while being hard-pressed to finance the construction of protective dikes.[61]

Global environmental disaster confronts the world's nations with an enormous task—and an unprecedented threat to *every* nation's security. The magnitude of efforts required—i.e., the capital needed for costly pollution control devices or new production technologies, the labor to plant trees, or the scientific know-how to develop substitute materials for CFCs—is largely unknown. According to an estimate by the Worldwatch Institute, however, the global community would have to expend a cumulative sum of about $774 billion during the final decade of this century to turn around adverse trends in four priority areas: protecting topsoil on croplands from further erosion, reforesting the earth, raising energy efficiency, and developing renewable sources of energy. This sum is equivalent to just under 10 percent of annual world military spending. Still, most Third World countries do not possess the resources needed either to cope with or remedy large-scale environmental degradation. At the March 1989 London ozone conference, for example, China and India suggested that industrialized countries should offer developing nations technical and financial support to develop CFC substitutes if they want them to join an international ozone protocol that phases out CFC production by the end of the century.[62]

Resource conflicts—struggles over access to and control over land, water, energy, and minerals—have historically lent themselves, at least in the view of competing governments, to military solutions. But what was once a zero-sum game—to the victor belong the spoils—has become transformed into a no-win situation as environmental threats have become more prominent and global in scope. Technologically sophisticated though they may be, military means cannot reverse resource depletion or restore lost ecological balance.

Reflecting on the true dimensions of national security, Wendell Berry, noted American writer and farmer, has asked: "To what point . . . do we defend from foreign enemies a country that we are destroying ourselves? In spite of all our propagandists can do, the foreign threat inevitably seems diminished when our air is unsafe to breathe, when our drinking water is unsafe to drink, when our rivers carry tonnages of topsoil that make light of the freight they carry in boats, when our forests are dying from air pollution and acid rain, and when we ourselves are sick from poisons in the air. Who *are* the enemies of this country?"[63]

Not only do military means contribute nothing to achieving environmental security, they detract from it in a variety of ways. Modern warfare entails large-scale environmental destruction; nuclear war, with its potential for massive and indiscriminate devastation, destruction of the ozone layer, and triggering of "nuclear winter," is the ultimate threat to the global environment. But even peacetime military operations—the production and testing of conventional and nuclear weapons, the conduct of maneuvers, and the generation of military-specific wastes—involve activities that imperil both the natural environment and the health of workers and nearby residents, a fact recently underscored by new revelations about the pervasive safety and environmental problems in the U.S. nuclear weapons industry. Again there is the irony that the pursuit of military might is such a costly endeavor that it drains away the resources urgently needed to protect against the environmental perils that are most likely to jeopardize national security.[64]

From Military to Environmental Alliances

In the face of transnational environmental problems of such magnitude, national responses are likely to prove fruitless without international cooperation. One of the obstacles to such cooperation is that national interests are not necessarily convergent: neither the harm of environmental degradation nor the benefits arising from protective measures are equally distributed. In addition, the capability of individual countries to shoulder the financial burden of remedial policies may differ considerably. And environmental awareness—and thus public pressure on governments to act—has developed much earlier and more strongly in some countries than in others. *Our Common Future*, the report of the World Commission on Environment and Development (the Brundtland Commission), put the dilemma succinctly: "The Earth is one but the world is not. We all depend on one biosphere for sustaining our lives. Yet each community, each country, strives for survival and prosperity with little regard for its impact on others."[65]

Fearful of setting far-reaching precedents, governments are often reluctant to relinquish any of their hard-won sovereign rights. At a conference of European environmental ministers to work out a cleanup program for the Rhine, France, Switzerland, and West Germany objected to a Dutch recommendation for international inspection of suspected pollution sites, arguing it would violate national sovereignty. West Germany similarly refused to consent to a proposal that would have entrusted the Secretariat of the United Nations Economic Commission for Europe with inspection of sources of sulfur dioxide pollution in Europe. Brazil, suddenly exposed to international pressure to halt the destruction of the Amazon rain forest, successfully resisted the proposed formation of an international environmental agency that it feared could intervene in what it sees as its internal affairs.[66]

But absolute sovereignty is not a workable concept. Exclusively national policies are ill-suited for a world that faces border-transcending environmental destruction of an unprecedented scope. But limits to national sovereignty are more often recognized in solemn declarations than in practical policies. The 1972 U.N. Conference on the Human Environment, for example, declared that all states have the responsibility to ensure that activities within their jurisdiction or control do not cause damage to the environment of other countries. Environmental security depends critically on a pragmatic internationalism: coordinating policies with other countries where purely national efforts are condemned to failure. Otherwise, each country is left at the mercy of others' actions.

As awareness of the transnational character of environmental degradation has grown and remedies have become more urgent, an increasing number of bilateral agreements and international conventions have been concluded, with varying degrees of national commitment to their implementation and thus success. UNEP has helped shepherd many of those efforts. Its most celebrated achievement to date is the 1987 Montreal Protocol that calls for a 50-percent cut in CFC production by 1998. But UNEP's mandate remains limited, and there are no overarching, firmly established international mechanisms to address ecological problems. For example, several of UNEP's attempts to draft rules on international responsibility for transboundary environmental damage have failed to win acceptance.[67]

Transnational coordination of environmental policies can occasionally even be a two-edged sword. In the case of standards for automotive emissions, for example, the consensus-building process within the European Economic Community has resulted in norms dictated by the lowest common denominator and has inhibited individual member countries from taking stricter national action.[68]

The success of international environmental cooperation depends in large measure on bold and imaginative policies to bridge gaps between nations and to strike a sound balance between conflicting interests. One avenue is simply to take unilateral initiatives: in a departure from the format of formal international conferences and negotiations, for instance, one or more like-minded countries could commit themselves to reducing their fossil fuel consumption, phasing out CFC production, stopping ocean dumping, or taking other measures, and then invite other nations to adopt similar restraints. If reciprocated, such initiatives can generate a new phenomenon in international affairs—environmental alliances. Formed to act against

> "The success of environmental cooperation depends on bold and imaginative policies to bridge gaps between nations and to strike a sound balance between competing interests."

a common threat, these alliances could tie together nations that share ecosystems; countries that are geographically distant but bear primary responsibility for global environmental threats; or political, ideological, or military rivals that may have little else in common other than an interest in avoiding environmental catastrophes.

While they may not be referred to in these terms, such alliances are already becoming a reality. At the initiative of the Scandinavian nations, nine European countries and Canada formed in 1984 what is informally known as the "30-percent Club." Aware that vast amounts of airborne pollutants drift across national borders, these nations committed themselves to reducing their 1980 levels of sulfur dioxide emissions, a chief culprit in the formation of acid rain, by at least 30 percent by 1993. A total of 19 countries have joined the club so far. A similar pledge to cut nitrogen oxides by 30 percent by 1998 was made by 12 European nations in 1988.[69]

Environmental coalitions that cut across adversarial military alliances can fulfill a valuable role by strengthening the common interests of opposing camps. Europe has been divided into East and West for four decades now, but joint policies to cope with environmental threats are helping to break down barriers of ideology and barbed wire. Tanks and planes *might* fend off a military attack, but no remedy exists to repel the airborne and waterborne pollutants that cross borders with impunity. Cooperation between the two sides is even more crucial because Eastern Europe's economic backwardness, strangling foreign debt, and strong pressure on state factories to cut losses and generate profits have relegated the environment to secondary status. Most of these countries also lack money to import sophisticated Western pollution control equipment. Environmental cooperation across the East-West divide first became manifest in the 1979 Convention on Long-range Transboundary Air Pollution (which gave rise to the "30-percent Club"). While many economic and political hurdles remain to be overcome, both sides are now showing considerably greater interest in enhanced cooperation.[70]

Due to its unique geographic and political position in Central Europe, West Germany stands to gain the most from stepped-up East-West cooperation in environmental and other matters. To date, according to Helmut Schreiber of the Institute for European Environmental Policy in Bonn, West Germany has been the most active country in cultivating these contacts: it is party to 70 to 80 percent of the 100 or so bilateral environmental agreements between Eastern and Western European countries.[71]

Countries suffering strongly from "imported" pollution may want to consider offering technical or financial assistance for pollution control measures in the "exporting" country. One such specific alliance is evolving among the countries that share the Elbe. This river—severely polluted with cadmium, mercury, lead, phosphates, and nitrates—flows through heavily industrialized parts of Czechoslovakia and East Germany before streaming through Hamburg, West Germany, and emptying into the North Sea. Because West Germany has an obvious interest in seeing the river cleaned up, it is considering co-funding a water treatment plant in East Germany. The two German states recently set a precedent for such financial arrangements when they agreed to jointly pay for desalinizing the small Werra River. In addition, East Germany has in principle agreed to intensify water pollution control efforts in exchange for West German financial assistance.[72]

Similar deals are likely to become more common. The Netherlands and West Germany shared in the costs of French pollution control measures for the Rhine. Comparable agreements concerning air pollution are still rare. However, West Germany agreed to pay for some sulfur dioxide scrubbers on Czechoslovakian power plants in an effort to reduce the air pollution wafting across the border, and it will probably also assist East Germany in the same manner.[73]

To have maximum impact, co-funding schemes will need to be extended to Poland and Hungary, which contribute strongly to European pollution but whose severe economic troubles prevent them from adequately investing in environmental protection. Such financial support is now under consideration within the framework of another emerging environmental coalition around the Baltic Sea.

> "The newfound urgency to counteract global
> environmental problems may also bring
> change in U.S.-Soviet relations."

Denmark, Finland, East and West Germany, Poland, the Soviet Union, and Sweden are beginning to coordinate measures to clean up the heavily polluted waterway. Sweden proposes to study the establishment of a European Environment Fund that would promote and finance international cooperation for reducing transboundary emissions.[74]

The newfound urgency to counteract global environmental problems may also bring change in U.S.-Soviet relations. As early as 1972, the military superpowers signed an Agreement on Cooperation in the Field of Environmental Protection. But activities carried out under the accord have been starved for funds. Nonetheless, without governmental sponsorship, scientists from the Soviet Union and the United States have begun to exchange data and viewpoints with regard to the greenhouse effect, in an effort dubbed "greenhouse glasnost." On a more official level, the U.S. and Soviet academies of science recently formed a joint Interacademy Committee on Global Ecology.[75]

A unique environmental alliance is shaping up in war-torn Central America. The region's governments agreed in 1988 to establish a series of "peace parks"—designed to preserve the region's fast-disappearing rain forests and to help promote sustainable development—straddling the borders of Costa Rica, El Salvador, Guatemala, Honduras, Nicaragua, and Panama. Nicaraguan official Lorenzo Cardenal hopes these reserves will become "a worldwide model of sustainable tropical forest development." Within the wider effort of the Central American countries to disentangle themselves from the legacy of many years of warfare and confrontation in the region, the peace parks offer an alternative vision for the border regions that hitherto have been military staging grounds and fields of battle. According to Jim Thorsell of the International Union for the Conservation of Nature, worldwide there are currently 68 border parks involving 66 countries. The concept of border-straddling parks that would not only serve as nature preserves but also as demilitarized buffer zones may soon take root in other regions of the globe. Additional proposals for peace parks have been made for border areas between Greece and Turkey, North and South Korea, Cameroon and Nigeria, Laos, Kampuchea and Vietnam, Pakistan and China, and Egypt and Sudan.[76]

Ultimately, national security depends on *all* countries becoming part of a global environmental coalition. In June 1988, the prime ministers of Norway and Canada called for an international "Law of the Air" analogous to the Law of the Sea—a treaty to protect the atmosphere from ozone depletion and the buildup of greenhouse gases. They envision the creation of a world atmosphere fund, financed by a tax on fossil fuel consumption in the industrial countries, which would provide the financial support for improving energy efficiency, switching to more benign fuels, developing acceptable substitutes for CFCs, and taking other remedial and preventive actions. While an innovative concept, making a Law of the Air treaty a reality will require many years of intense international bargaining. But steps in the right direction are already being taken. In November 1988, the Intergovernmental Panel on Climate Change was created to hammer out a global accord limiting the release of greenhouse gases; UNEP Director Mostafa Tolba hopes a treaty will be ready for signature by 1992. Meanwhile, after it became clear that the Montreal Protocol provisions are inadequate to save the ozone layer, the United States and the European Community committed themselves to phasing out CFC production by the year 2000, inviting all other nations to follow suit.[77]

The success of international environmental policies depends on the collaboration of those countries that contribute most to environmental degradation. One of the worst offenders has been the Soviet Union, but under Gorbachev's leadership the Kremlin is gradually becoming a more responsible player in environmental matters. In a speech to the U.N. General Assembly, Soviet Foreign Minister Eduard Shevardnadze acknowledged that "the biosphere recognizes no division into blocs, alliances, or systems. All share the same climatic system and no one is in a position to build his own isolated and independent line of environmental defense." Shevardnadze proposed to turn UNEP "into an Environmental Council capable

> "Ultimately, national security depends on all countries becoming part of a global environmental coalition."

taking effective decisions to ensure ecological security." In a July 1988 communiqué, the Soviet Union and its Warsaw Pact allies said they are prepared to negotiate with other countries a binding code of conduct for international environmental relations. This is a startling about-face for countries that used to claim that their economic system was free of the environmental troubles besetting the capitalist West. So far, however, the Soviet Union's bold rhetoric is not being backed up by real commitments. At the March 1989 London ozone conference, for instance, the Soviets refused to go along with a CFC phaseout, and they are stalling on making significant commitments to reduce global warming as well.[78]

Grassroots pressure continues to play an important role in pushing governments to stem environmental degradation. In widely divergent ways, environmental groups have sought not only to influence the policies of their own governments and corporations, but also, by linking up with their counterparts abroad, those of foreign governments and of international organizations such as the World Bank. The Rainforest Action Network, for instance, is pressuring development banks not to fund projects that destroy the remaining rain forests. The Environmental Project on Central America is organizing American support for the Central American peace parks. Conservation International, the Nature Conservancy, and the World Wildlife Fund have pioneered innovative financial arrangements known as debt-for-nature swaps. Survival International is concerned with preserving the habitat on which endangered peoples depend, and Brazil's Amazon Indians and groups of rubber tappers, in turn, seek to gain support abroad in their struggle to save their lands. Greenpeace has developed a truly globe-spanning network of activists mobilized on a wide range of issues.[79]

Environmental links across the East-West divide on the grassroots level are still in their infancy. But Friends of the Earth and Greenpeace, among others, are busy building contacts with the nascent Eastern European and Soviet environmental movements. A number of private Soviet and American groups, meanwhile, emphasize that a healthy environment is an inalienable human right. Their goal is to formulate a Citizens' Treaty on Ecological Security, which they hope could become a vehicle for creating a "global culture of ecological responsibility" and to help establish binding principles governing ecological relations among countries.[80]

For grassroots groups to have a more effective voice in transnational environmental matters, individuals and non-governmental organizations need to play a greater role not only in domestic decision-making processes, but also in those of countries whose activities directly impinge on their own nation's environmental security. The Scandinavian countries have moved into the forefront in this regard. Article 3 of the 1974 Nordic Convention on the Protection of the Environment gives citizens of all signatory states affected by

> environmentally harmful activities in another contracting state . . . the right to bring before the appropriate court or administrative authority of that state the question of the permissibility of such activities, including the question of measures to prevent damage, and to appeal against the decision of the court or the administrative authority to the same extent and on the same terms as a legal entity of the state in which the activities are being carried out.

The convention applies the same provisions to compensation for transborder pollution damage. Sweden and Norway have asked other European countries to grant this right as well, but a recommendation by the OECD Council in the seventies to establish the "equal legal access" principle in member countries foundered on the objection that such a right constitutes an undue interference in domestic affairs.[81]

Rapidly growing awareness of environmental issues by grassroots leaders and policymakers brings with it the hope that environmental threats to security can be put much higher on the agenda of all nations. Even though the biosphere is still a rather new element in international relations, environmental diplomacy is already moving to center stage.

From National to Global Security

Reversing environmental degradation confronts the global community with an unprecedented need for stepped-up international cooperation. This monumental task cannot be accomplished without putting an end to the arms race, which claims so much of decision makers' attention and devours so much of the resources needed to halt the danger to the planet. (See Table 8.)

To release a significant share of the resources now devoted to the military, nations need to move in new directions in security policy. The present course has been an outstanding failure, and more than arms control will be needed for the future. Instead of putting a brake on military competition, previous superpower agreements have served as a smokescreen for a continuing arms buildup: tailored to establish weak limits for aging or redundant weapons systems, they also stimulated the development and deployment of more-sophisticated technologies.

The first round of strategic arms limitation talks, SALT I, for example, provided an opportunity to ban multiple-warhead missiles (MIRVs). At the time of the accord, the Soviet Union had not deployed any MIRVs, while the United States had 832 in place. But rather than remove these and prohibit any future deployments, SALT I permitted a total of 2,640 multiple-warhead missiles for both sides. The SALT I and II treaties established warhead ceilings much higher than existing arsenals, thus allowing the superpowers to add almost 13,000 warheads to their strategic nuclear stockpiles.[82]

The proposed Strategic Arms Reductions Talks (START) accord would cut strategic nuclear weapons by 30–35 percent, returning warhead numbers to the level prevalent in the late seventies. But numerical limits alone—however deep a cut may be envisioned—will fail to arrest the most dynamic aspects of the arms race. Military strategists always discover new security threats and weapons gaps to justify the deployment of new arms. Though hailed as a radical proposal,

Table 8: Trade-offs Between Military and Social or Environmental Priorities

Military Priority	Cost	Social/Environmental Priority
Trident II submarine and F-16 jet fighter programs	$100,000,000,000	Estimated clean-up cost for the 3,000 worst hazardous waste dumps in the United States
Stealth bomber program	$68,000,000,000	Two-thirds of estimated costs to meet U.S. clean water goals by 2000
Requested SDI funding fiscal year 1988–92	$39,000,000,000	Disposal of highly radioactive waste in the United States (non-military)
2 weeks of world military expenditure	$30,000,000,000	Annual cost of the proposed U.N. Water and Sanitation Decade
German outlays for military procurement and R&D, FY 1985	$10,750,000,000	Estimated clean-up costs for West German sector of the North Sea
Approx. 4 days of global military spending	$8,000,000,000	Action Plan over 5 years to save the world's tropical forests
Development cost for Midgetman ICBM	$6,000,000,000	Annual cost to cut U.S. sulfur dioxide emissions by 8–12 million tons/year to combat acid rain
Approx. 2 days of global military spending	$4,800,000,000	Annual cost of proposed U.N. Action Plan to halt Third World desertification over 20 years
6 months of U.S. outlays for nuclear warheads, FY 1986	$4,000,000,000	U.S. government outlays for energy efficiency, FY 1980–87

Military Priority	Cost	Social/Environmental Priority
SDI research, FY 1987	$3,700,000,000	Enough funds to build a solar power system serving a city of 200,000
3 weeks of military spending of countries with literacy rates of 50 percent or less	$2,400,000,000	Additional UNESCO budget needs, over a decade, to eliminate illiteracy worldwide
10 days of European Economic Community military spending	$2,000,000,000	Annual cost to clean up hazardous waste sites in 10 European Economic Community countries by the year 2000
1 Trident submarine	$1,400,000,000	5-year child immunization program against 6 deadly diseases, preventing 1 million deaths a year
3 B-1B bombers	$680,000,000	U.S. government spending on renewable energy, FY 1983–85
2 months of Ethiopian military spending	$50,000,000	Annual cost of proposed U.N. Anti-desertification Plan for Ethiopia
1 nuclear weapon test	$12,000,000	Installation of 80,000 hand pumps to give Third World villages access to safe water
1-hour operating cost, B-1B bomber	$21,000	Community-based maternal health care in 10 African villages to reduce maternal deaths by half in one decade

Source: Worldwatch Institute, based on various sources.

a START treaty as currently envisioned would not slow the tide of increasingly expensive weapons planned or on the drawing board because it does not impose any constraints on further technical improvements and refinements.[83]

Terminating the arms race and releasing substantial resources needed to address pressing social, economic, and environmental problems would require a cutoff of fissionable materials production and a comprehensive curb on further development, production, testing, and deployment of new warheads and delivery systems, coupled with significant reductions in existing nuclear and conventional armaments. While technological advances allow much more reliable verification of such measures from outside a country's borders, the unprecedented Soviet willingness to accept intrusive verification procedures has also removed one of the major political obstacles.[84]

A shutdown of plants producing the plutonium and highly enriched uranium used in nuclear warheads was actually favored by U.S. officials from 1957 to 1970 but was rejected by Moscow. A new opportunity exists now, however, for implementing such a proposal. Pollution and safety concerns have forced the temporary closing of scores of U.S. nuclear weapons production facilities, and there are indications that the Soviet Union faces similar problems. The Los Alamos National Laboratory said in June 1988 that "Soviet military production reactors are old, obsolete, and unsafe. They will be shut down soon." Indeed, President Gorbachev recently announced that the Soviet Union would end its production of enriched uranium in 1989 and reduce its output of plutonium by the end of 1990. A U.S.-Soviet moratorium on the production of weapons-grade material could keep all remaining plants shut while a permanent ban is negotiated. A ban on production of tritium—a radioactive form of hydrogen that boosts the blast of nuclear bombs—could be a corollary to a prohibition of plutonium production. Banning the military use of tritium, according to Paul Leventhal of the Washington, D.C.-based Nuclear Control Institute, would set a steady pace for disarmament: it decays at a constant rate and must be replenished regularly to maintain the explosive power of nuclear warheads.[85]

"Once the momentum of the arms race is broken, attention can be directed toward the difficult but crucial task of reversing the process."

Once the momentum of the arms race is broken, attention can be directed toward the difficult but crucial task of reversing the armament process. It has been a quarter-century since the superpowers seriously contemplated general and complete disarmament. In 1961, Washington and Moscow agreed on the McCloy-Zorin Joint Statement of Agreed Principles for Disarmament Negotiations, the terms of which were unanimously adopted by the U.N. General Assembly that September. The statement contained guidelines for multilateral negotiations to design and implement an international disarmament program. In accordance with these principles, in 1962 the administration of President John F. Kennedy presented a treaty outline to an international conference and distributed its provisions in a document entitled *Blueprint for the Peace Race*. By late 1963, however, that approach was shunted aside in favor of "arms control"—a term that has come to mean a managed version of the arms race.[86]

Almost three decades later, the merits of disarmament are worth reconsidering. Recognizing the dire military and economic implications of the arms race, Gorbachev presented a plan in January 1986 to rid the world of all nuclear weapons by the end of the century. Meanwhile, Marcus Raskin, a former member of President Kennedy's National Security Council, now a senior fellow at the Institute for Policy Studies in Washington, D.C., has launched an effort to revive the McCloy-Zorin Principles. He has formulated, and submitted to American and Soviet analysts for comment, a detailed and careful draft treaty that spells out a 15-year process for disbanding the world's armed forces, eliminating all stockpiles of weapons and their delivery vehicles, and converting arms industries to civilian use. In painstaking detail, it enunciates the legal and institutional provisions, mechanisms, safeguards, and verification procedures necessary for the successful implementation of a disarmament treaty.[87]

The McCloy-Zorin principles and the Raskin draft treaty provide a fresh departure from the incrementalism that has hampered attempts to make the world more secure. However, if this vision of a world without war is to be translated into political reality, it needs to be accompanied by specific steps to reach that goal. Governments and citizens alike need a road map that gives them a measure of confidence that they can navigate this largely uncharted territory. The conventional wisdom among government officials, journalists, educators, and others holds that "living with nuclear weapons"—the control of arms rather than their abolition—is the best we can hope for. Four decades of cold war have reinforced this notion to the point where it seems unrealistic to many people to envision a disarmed world. Albert Einstein's famous remark that "the unleashed power of the atom has changed everything save our modes of thinking" still rings true today.[88]

A world in which the use of force becomes increasingly delegitimized is not a utopian dream. Just as the abolition of slavery once seemed unrealistic, disarmament too can come to be the normal state of international affairs. A disarmed world is not necessarily defenseless, as Harvard's Gene Sharp has shown with his thought-provoking advocacy of a non-violent, or "civilian-based," defense. In an age in which the destructive power of modern military technology allows no effective protection, the security of a nation may be better safeguarded, and a potential aggressor better deterred, by the prospect of the organized non-military resistance and non-cooperation of the entire population.[89]

Arms negotiations seldom provide a forum for the kind of innovative and bold approaches that seem essential to genuine disarmament. An alternative approach, which has come to be known as "independent initiatives," may prove more fruitful. Taken outside the realm of formal and often secretive bargaining sessions, they seek to bring the weight of world public opinion to bear on disarmament. Independent initiatives are guided by a simple principle, one similar to that outlined in the previous section as a basis for the formation of informal environmental alliances. Either the United States or the Soviet Union, for example, might publicly announce it will refrain from testing and deploying any new nuclear weapons for a specified period, say one year. If reciprocated by the other side, that constraint could be extended for an indefinite period, and at a later point be codified in a formal accord. The superpowers have accumulated

"With the help of independent initiatives, an alternative security system could materialize."

such overkill that they could easily take initial steps without immediate reciprocation: even if one were to cut back its strategic nuclear arsenal by 90 percent, it could still inflict unacceptable damage on the other after suffering a first strike itself.[90]

Such an approach is not confined to theory. A voluntary nuclear test moratorium begun by the Soviet Union in 1958 was observed by the then three nuclear powers for three years before testing resumed at a high rate. When President Kennedy announced another unilateral moratorium on atmospheric nuclear testing in 1963, the Soviets responded positively. That helped lead to the Limited Test Ban Treaty later that year.[91]

Mikhail Gorbachev has revived this approach in an effort to break the arms control stalemate. Among other measures, he instituted unilateral moratoria on testing nuclear explosives and anti-satellite weapons, reduced the size of Soviet naval forces in the Pacific by perhaps as much as half, and announced that all Soviet chemical weapons stockpiles would be destroyed. Despite a remarkable thaw in East-West relations, however, his initiatives have not been reciprocated. A constructive American response—testing the sincerity of Soviet proposals and presenting similar offers—might create a positive dynamic in the superpower relationship and build the trust necessary to move toward disarmament. The administration of President George Bush now has a historic opportunity to terminate the arms race and fundamentally alter the superpower relationship.[92]

With the help of independent initiatives, an alternative security system could gradually materialize. Although most governments employ not a single person for the purpose of designing such a system and thinking through its implications, some nongovernmental groups have put their imagination to work. A debate over alternative defense has simmered for many years within academic and peace movement circles. It has gathered momentum in Europe, as denuclearization and a reduction of conventional forces have suddenly emerged as serious options in the wake of the 1987 U.S.-Soviet Intermediate-range Nuclear Forces Treaty. A "nonprovocative defense" would involve a fundamental restructuring of the armed forces—weapons, personnel, and strategies—so that they can defend but lack the ability to attack. This implies clear limits on the range and destructive power of weapons, as well as restrictions on the size and mobility of troops. It may be difficult to draw the sometimes fine line between offensive and defensive characteristics, but the litmus test is whether a defensive system augments a country's security *without* increasing the threat to other nations' security.[93]

The discussion in Europe stretches across a fairly diverse spectrum of options and proposals, ranging from schemes focusing on little more than a restructuring of military hardware ("transarmament") to more sophisticated and ambitious propositions that seek to transcend the East-West divide, and eventually dismantle the military blocs, by nurturing the common security interests of the opposing sides.[94]

In the eighties, alternative defense has, in the words of Hal Harvey, former director of the security program at the Rocky Mountain Institute, "graduated from theory to politics." The Danish parliament has established a research center to study nonprovocative defense, and the Social Democratic Party in West Germany and the Labor Party in the United Kingdom are advocating such policies.[95]

Similar concepts have entered the vocabulary of Soviet military and party leaders. Mikhail Gorbachev has coined the term "reasonable sufficiency" to guide the transition of Soviet military doctrine from offense to defense. The Soviet leader underscored his willingness to accept asymmetrical reductions where Soviet forces enjoy a numerical advantage over Western armies in a dramatic speech before the United Nations General Assembly in December 1988. Gorbachev announced major unilateral troop and tank cuts in Eastern Europe and the European part of the Soviet Union, followed by a restructuring of the remaining Soviet forces in Eastern Europe, so that they will become "clearly defensive." Moscow's Warsaw Pact allies (except Romania) subsequently disclosed they would reduce their own military spending and the size of their armed forces. Finally, at the new East-West talks on conventional arms reductions in Europe, the Warsaw Pact reiterated its July 1988 proposal for a negotiated, three-step conventional arms reduction process leading to strictly defensive postures on both sides. Thus, it appears that in the nineties alternative security may further progress from politics to reality.[96]

Superpower movement toward disarmament is important not only because the United States and the Soviet Union account for more than half of global military expenditures and control by far the largest arsenals, but also because an unfettered arms race between them indirectly lends legitimacy to other countries' efforts to acquire nuclear weapons. As long as possession of a nuclear arsenal seems to have political or military value, conferring special status and diplomatic leverage, it is of little surprise that countries such as Argentina, Brazil, India, Iraq, Israel, Pakistan, and South Africa have crossed or seek to cross the nuclear threshold. As part of the bargain to prevent the spread of nuclear weapons—the Nuclear Non-proliferation Treaty of 1970—the nuclear "have-nots" agreed to forego possession of such arms in return for a commitment from the "haves" to move seriously toward disarmament. That promise remains unfulfilled.[97]

Because conflicts and wars in the Third World arise from a multitude of causes, there are frequently no easy solutions to the conflicts. Real security within and among all nations cannot be achieved without addressing the manifold and fundamental inequities that fuel violent disputes: there can be no lasting peace without justice. However, in numerous cases, Third World conflicts are exacerbated by the involvement of the United States, the Soviet Union, or other outside powers. An absence of foreign intervention may not be enough to guarantee smooth conflict resolution, but at least it removes an additional complicating factor.

For the superpowers, the lessons of Vietnam and Afghanistan, and to a lesser extent, Central America and Lebanon, suggest that military intervention has reached the point of diminishing returns. Either the United States or the Soviet Union could offer to refrain from sending armed forces or weapons into any other country, in return for similar self-restraint from the other superpower. Such a nonintervention policy was in effect endorsed in early 1988 by a panel of former and current American and Soviet officials in a report on "The Requirements for Stable Coexistence in United States–Soviet Relations."[98]

The second stage of a nonintervention policy would involve the withdrawal of foreign troops now stationed abroad. President Gorbachev, for example, proposed removing Soviet naval forces from Cam Ranh Bay and other facilities in Vietnam, if the United States in return agrees to abandon its military bases in the Philippines. Gorbachev's proposal was rejected by U.S. officials because the United States would lose access to bases that are larger than those controlled by the Soviet Union. However, the principle that the United States enthusiastically endorsed in the context of European conventional force reductions—i.e., the side that holds a numerical advantage in armaments should make larger cutbacks—could very well be applied in this case.[99]

The best hope for impartial conflict resolution rests with the United Nations. The history of U.N. peacekeeping efforts shows that the organization has been an effective conciliator of conflicts that do not involve the major powers. Even though the high hopes invested in United Nations peacekeeping efforts have largely been disappointed during the first four decades of its existence, the organization's reputation has improved sharply in recent months.[100]

The changing Soviet attitude toward the U.N. is a particularly encouraging development, as reflected in Soviet payment of past membership dues, Moscow's proposals for a U.N. peacekeeping fleet in the Persian Gulf, its acceptance of U.N.-mediated talks that led to the withdrawal of Soviet troops from Afghanistan, and its pressure on allies like Angola, Ethiopia, and Vietnam to seek negotiated settlements of the conflicts in which they have been embroiled for more than a decade. If the Bush administration decides to reverse

"The best hope for impartial conflict resolution lies with the United Nations."

President Reagan's retreat from multilateralism, the United Nations could finally overcome the paralysis imposed on it by the cold war and become what its founders envisioned: an organization at the center of a collective security system.

Meanwhile, the United Nations has achieved numerous recent successes in conflict resolution, and its peacekeeping forces won the 1988 Nobel Peace Prize. This decade has seen numerous conflicts around the globe that seem to have no victors but only vanquished— the Iran-Iraq war, Soviet forces pitched against the Afghan mujahedin, the Vietnamese occupation of Kampuchea, and the struggle between the Sahrawi people and Morocco over control of the Western Sahara. The U.N. has played a key role in defusing these conflicts, and there is also hope that U.N. soldiers and observers will play a crucial role in Namibia's transition to independence, despite the outbreak of new fighting and charges by Third World countries that the United Nations has fumbled the transition process. Sheer exhaustion and war weariness have driven these various combatants to embrace the U.N. as a peacemaker, and U.N.-sponsored cease-fire negotiations have proven to be a face-saving way out of a stalemated conflict.

But if the world body's current peacekeeping efforts continue to be successful, it can capitalize on its new-found prestige to cope with an even more daunting challenge: to move from organizing cease-fires and creating buffer zones between hostile camps to preventing the outbreak of hostilities in the first place. U.N. Secretary-General Javier Perez de Cuellar created the Office for Research and the Collection of Information in 1987, which is charged with helping to recognize conflicts before they erupt and trying to defuse them. In the future, armed conflict may well be prevented by having either unarmed observers or peacekeeping forces already in place. Indeed, as part of a proposal for a comprehensive security system, the Soviet Union recently urged the United Nations to set up "observation posts in explosive areas of the world." Deputy Foreign Minister Vladimir F. Petrovsky suggested that any country seeking to protect itself from outside interference should be able to call on the U.N. to send observer teams to patrol its borders.[101]

In 1983, Nicaragua called for an eight-nation Latin American contingent to patrol its border with Honduras to deter incursions by the U.S.-backed Contras, a proposal echoed by Honduran Foreign Minister Lopez Contreras in 1988. In March 1989, the Central American governments finally came to a tentative agreement to establish a small peacekeeping force of only 160 soldiers. If a U.N. team or another international force had been available in the early eighties, it might have avoided some of the bloodshed in the region. It would also have been much cheaper for all parties involved. The Pentagon estimates that a force of 1,300 observers could monitor the borders separating Nicaragua from Honduras, El Salvador, and Costa Rica for less than $40 million a year. By contrast, the United States spends some $3 billion annually to project military force into the region, and the Central American countries together spend another $1 billion on their armies.[102]

Currently, U.N. peacekeeping forces are created for specific missions, on an ad hoc basis. They are composed of contingents of national armed forces that can be withdrawn by their governments on short notice. The world body's members may want to consider a more permanent peacekeeping force. To solidify the impartiality of such a force—and therefore its acceptability—it should ideally consist of individually recruited persons, trained in the unique skills of peacekeeping, and whose loyalty to the United Nations is not in question.[103]

Annual outlays for the seven current U.N. peacekeeping operations come to about $380 million currently. A stepped-up role would require greater outlays. The organization may soon be spending $2 billion a year if it assumes an active role in Kampuchea, the Western Sahara, and southern Africa. That would still be less than what the world spends on the arms race in a single day.[104]

One reason governments resist disarmament is that they not only distrust each other, but habitually equate an opponent's intentions with its capabilities (which are always assessed in so-called "worst-case scenarios"). An international satellite monitoring agency—first proposed in 1962—could help build greater trust. Undertaking modest tasks at first, it might eventually provide impartial information to verify arms treaties, confirm or deny alleged border violations, deter surprise attacks, monitor cease-fires, and assist U.N. peacekeeping missions. According to a U.N. General Assembly study, start-up and operating costs would be well under 1 percent of annual world military expenditures.[105]

The General Assembly is already considering the establishment of a more limited monitoring center that, for the time being, would not involve satellite monitoring. Canada has proposed a satellite system called PAXSAT specifically designed to verify conventional force reductions in Europe. In the United States, Representative Robert Mrazek (D-New York) has introduced a bill in Congress to investigate how satellite monitoring can increase international security and stability.[106]

Governments cannot always be expected to initiate daring new disarmament policies. Robert Johansen has aptly said: "To expect the world's most powerful governments, without outside pressure, to build a new security system where those states now militarily weak would gain influence relative to the states now militarily strong, is like expecting a divine right king to lead the revolution for democracy and for abolition of the throne."[107]

The greatest hope for reining in the arms race lies in the vocal and insistent pressure that has emerged from the grassroots. People everywhere are less and less inclined to leave the responsibility for defining security to governments. Their agendas range from traditional peace movement actions to innovative acts of citizen diplomacy. The Natural Resources Defense Council, by persuading Soviet authorities to let it establish seismic monitoring stations near the nuclear testing grounds at Semipalatinsk, helped compel the Reagan administration to reopen talks with Moscow about nuclear test ban verification. The Institute for Policy Studies has initiated an ambitious Real Security Education Project, which brings labor, church, and peace movement representatives together in workshops that explore the manifold dimensions of security. The Campaign for Peace and Democracy/East and West, the European Nuclear Disarmament Campaign, and activists from the West German Green Party, among others, are busy building the basis for a "détente from below"—a grassroots alliance of peace and human rights groups straddling the military blocs in Europe.

To be successful, strategies to reverse the arms race need to address not only the roots of military insecurity, but also the economic and political reasons for military competition. Keeping nations in a state of constant war preparation gives politicians, bureaucrats, and generals political power and command over a sizable share of resources even in a democratic society. Due to generous cost-plus contracts, arms manufacturers often derive larger profits from their operations than their counterparts in civilian industry. Meanwhile, military workers, and their families and communities, are worried about disarmament because it threatens their livelihoods.[108]

A well-planned economic conversion process would not only address many of these concerns but facilitate the rechanneling of resources from military to civilian uses. Conversion is a critical component in reordering the priorities of a nation's security policy. The first step is to identify existing innovative and productive capabilities—the capital, raw materials, machinery, and human skills and expertise—now tied up in military-related production. Second, a mechanism must be developed for rechanneling these capabilities back into civilian use. Legislation proposed by U.S. Representative Ted Weiss (D-New York), for example, would create an institutional framework for national conversion planning and would mandate the formation of local alternative-use committees in every military plant, base, or laboratory. These committees would develop a blueprint for civilian product development and marketing. The bill further provides for occupational retraining of managers, engineers, and workers to help them adapt to the requirements of the civilian market.[109]

> "To be successful, strategies to reverse the arms race need to address not only the roots of military insecurity, but also the economic and political reasons for military competition."

Conversion could also be a means of freeing money and technical skills needed to reverse environmental degradation. Specific proposals have sought to make the specialized skills at military bases and laboratories directly available to addressing environment-related problems. For example, in 1978 the University of California Nuclear Weapons Labs Conversion Project studied the potential for switching the Lawrence Livermore Laboratory—an important weapons-development facility—to work on alternative energy projects. A similar proposal envisioned transforming the Fort Detrick biological warfare facility in Maryland into a center for cancer and related biomedical research. Lacking political support and the framework of a broad national conversion strategy, these proposals never matured beyond the stage of feasibility studies.[110]

The United States gathered practical conversion experience at the close of World War II, when 30 percent of its GNP was transferred from the war industry to civilian uses within a few years. Today, China provides another example. As a share of GNP, military spending has declined from about 13 percent during the seventies to a low of 7 percent in 1985. In that year, the country decided to slice its 4-million-strong armed forces by one-fourth and to use part of the military-industrial capacity to manufacture civilian goods. Civilian production now accounts for 38 percent of the output of China's 30,000 "military" factories.[111]

Even the Soviet Union now seems ready to tackle the conversion process. In his U.N. speech, President Gorbachev promised to "draw up, as an experiment, conversion plans for two or three defense plants" in the course of 1989. He further added that "it is desirable that all states, in the first place major military powers, should submit to the United Nations their national conversion plans." The cuts of close to 20 percent in Soviet arms production announced by Gorbachev at the beginning of this year will put the new Soviet policy to the test.[112]

Conclusion

In many crucial respects, nations are no longer the sole masters of their destinies. Production, trade, investment, modern communications, and tourism are now inherently global in scale, rapidly transforming this diverse planet into an interlinked unit. What happens in practically any part of the world can affect remote areas elsewhere. This interdependence in economic, military, and environmental affairs has already begun to erode traditional notions of security and even national sovereignty itself.

Military, economic, and ecological developments increasingly seem to dictate a global community of interests. But because interdependence has come about by default rather than by design it does not automatically generate the political will needed for greater international cooperation. The world is still plagued by enormous inequalities in power, wealth, and capacity to influence global affairs. Indeed, divided loyalties, conflicting interests, and rivalries have left humanity fragmented along political, ethnic, religious, and socioeconomic dividing lines.

Nations have "outgrown" their borders, but the structures of nation-states remain firmly in place. Like membranes, national borders are at times porous, at times impermeable. They cannot stem the flow of goods, money, or ideas, nor that of polluted air or water. Still, they often repel appeals for common approaches to shared problems. Visions of a common security system are still held in check by the reality of national rivalry and common insecurity. Thus, paradoxically, we live in two seemingly incompatible worlds: an Earth without firm boundaries, and a world that retains many of its borders.

Greater security for all nations depends on creating a more stable and equitable basis for their economic and environmental relationships. In economic relations among countries, both independence and interdependence have their merits. It is important for a nation to be as self-sufficient as possible in "strategic" items such as food and energy supplies. Improved efficiency not only reduces reliance on imports but also helps ease international competition for scarce natural resources and the resulting potential for conflict. On the other hand, increased economic interdependence in areas with a potential for mutual gain are desirable. The experience of France and Germany—which fought against each other for centuries but which are now close allies and trading partners—suggests that the greater the stake in economic cooperation, the more unthinkable war becomes. Disrupting the relationship promises far fewer benefits than does strengthening it.[113]

"Environmental security" offers a more fruitful basis for cooperation and security among nations than military security because it is both a positive and inclusive concept. Whereas military security offers at best the continuation of an uneasy status quo and at worst the prospect of annihilation, environmental security seeks to protect or to restore. While military security rests firmly on the competitive strength of individual countries at the direct expense of other nations, environmental security cannot be achieved unilaterally: it both requires and nurtures more stable and cooperative relationships among nations.

Reflecting on the opportunities for increased U.S.-Soviet cooperation in environmental and other matters, former U.S. Ambassador George Kennan, now a scholar at the Institute for Advanced Study in New Jersey, has argued that "in the very process of collaboration in a necessary and peaceful process, useful to all humanity, the neurotic impulses of military and political rivalry would be bound to be overshadowed; and the peoples might find, in the intermingling of their own creative efforts, a firmness of association which no other intergovernmental relationships could ever assure."[114]

The task of strengthening the economic and environmental dimensions of global security is as challenging as it is imperative. To succeed, no less than a fundamental re-examination of the assumptions that have guided national security policies in the postwar era is required. The profound transformations that our world is undergoing challenge the traditional conduct of diplomacy and the established forms of governance. Indeed, "national security" as such has become an outmoded concept: security is increasingly attained through the difficult process of global cooperation to create mechanisms for nonviolent dispute settlement and establish environmental alliances. As they look back, future generations may regard our recent obsession with national security maintained by force of arms as a curious historical diversion that distracted our energies from the most basic threats to human society.

Notes

1. Gene Sharp, *Making Europe Unconquerable: The Potential of Civilian-based Deterrence and Defense* (Cambridge, Mass.: Ballinger, 1985); Carolyn Stephenson, "Alternative International Security Systems: An Introduction," in Carolyn Stephenson (ed.), *Alternative Methods for International Security* (Lanham, Md.: University Press of America, 1982).

2. See, for example, Robin Luckham, "Myths and Realities of Security," in Burns H. Weston (ed.), *Toward Nuclear Disarmament and Global Security* (Boulder, Colo.: Westview, 1984).

3. Rita Tullberg, "World Military Expenditures," *Bulletin of Peace Proposals*, Vol. 17, No. 3–4, 1986; Ruth Leger Sivard, *World Military and Social Expenditures 1987–88* (Washington, D.C: World Priorities, 1988); military expenditures are likely to be understated for a number of reasons: highly aggregated budget categories make the identification of security-related outlays outside a defense ministry difficult or impossible, countries like Indonesia make heavy use of off-budget financing, military imports may be bartered for other goods (as practiced by Ethiopia, India, and Iraq); Nicole Ball, *Security and Economy in the Third World* (Princeton, N.J.: Princeton University Press, 1988).

4. United Nations, Center for Disarmament, Disarmament Study Series No. 5, *The Relationship Between Disarmament and Development* (New York: 1982), for estimate of world paramilitary forces; ILO estimate reported in United Nations General Assembly, *Report of the Secretary-General: Study on the Economic and Social Consequences of the Arms Race and Military Expenditures*, A/43/368 (New York: May 19, 1988); Mexican population from Population Reference Bureau, *1988 World Population Data Sheet* (Washington, D.C., 1988).

5. Arms transfer value is a Worldwatch Institute estimate, based on U.S. Arms Control and Disarmament Agency (ACDA), *World Military Expenditures and Arms Transfers 1987* (Washington, D.C.: U.S. Government Printing Office, March 1988); military grant aid allowed many Third World countries to procure otherwise unaffordable equipment during the fifties and sixties and to engage in war or "to avoid having to make political concessions necessary to settle long-standing disputes," according to Ball, *Security and Economy in the Third World*; Gary Thatcher, "Poison on the Wind" (four-part series on "The New Threat of Chemical and Biological Weapons—Part 1: The Poisons Spread"), *Christian Science Monitor*, December 13, 1988; Aaron Karp, "The Frantic Third World Quest for Ballistic Missiles," *Bulletin of the Atomic Scientists*, June 1988, for recent trends in chemical arms and ballistic missile proliferation.

6. Sivard, *World Military and Social Expenditures 1987–88*.

7. Ibid.

8. Brzezinski quoted in *New York Times*, January 18, 1981; Weinberger quoted in Jonathan Schell, *The Abolition* (New York: Alfred A. Knopf, 1984).

9. So-called MARVs can change their direction during flight (unlike current reentry vehicles, which follow a ballistic trajectory), earth-penetrating warheads would dig deep into the ground before exploding to destroy hidden command-and-control bunkers, "third generation" nuclear devices (like the neutron bomb, the x-ray laser, and electro-magnetic pulse weapons) and "exotic" weapons (like hypervelocity pellet weapons, microwave weapons, and optical frequency lasers) are being planned; Frank Barnaby, "Microelectronics and War," in John Tirman (ed.), *The Militarization of High Technology* (Cambridge, Mass.: Ballinger, 1984); for a detailed account of the trend toward war-fighting, see Michio Kaku and David Axelrod, *To Win a Nuclear War* (Boston: South End Press, 1987); The Commission on Integrated Long-term Strategy, *Discriminate Deterrence* (Washington, D.C.: U.S. Government Printing Office, January 1988).

10. Leonard S. Spector, "New Players in the Nuclear Game," *Bulletin of the Atomic Scientists*, January/February 1989.

11. Sivard, *World Military and Social Expenditures 1987–88*, for war statistics; Miroslav Nincic, *How War Might Spread to Europe* (Philadelphia: Taylor and Francis, 1985), for danger of global conflagration; Boulding quoted in Greg Mitchell, "Real Security. What Is It? How Can We Get It?" *Nuclear Times*, May/June 1986.

12. More than half the civilian deaths in recent hostilities, such as Afghanistan, Ethiopia, Mozambique, and the Sudan, resulted from war-related famine; Sivard, *World Military and Social Expenditures 1987–88*.

13. Ball, *Security and Economy in the Third World*.

14. Soedjatmoko, "Patterns of Armed Conflict in the Third World," *Alternatives*, Vol. 10, No. 4, 1985; Center for Defense Information, "A World At War—1983," *The Defense Monitor*, Vol. 12, No. 1, 1983; Ball, *Security and Economy in the Third World*.

15. Mohammed Ayoob, "The Iran-Iraq War and Regional Security in the Persian Gulf," *Alternatives*, Vol. 10, No. 4, 1985.

16. Robert C. Johansen, *Toward a Dependable Peace: A Proposal for an Appropriate Security System*, World Policy Paper No. 8 (New York: World Policy Institute, 1983).

17. Paul Kennedy, *The Rise and Fall of the Great Powers* (New York: Random House, 1987).

18. Lloyd Jeffry Dumas, *The Overburdened Economy* (Berkeley, Calif.: University of California Press, 1986), for a general discussion of relevance of GNP as an economic indicator.

19. Clyde H. Farnsworth, "Study Finds Soviet Output Is Stagnant," *New York Times*, April 25, 1988; "Budget Perestroika," *The Economist*, October 8, 1988; David Remnick, "Soviet Officials Detail Budget, Paint Grim Economic Picture," *Washington Post*, October, 28, 1988, and Nicholas Eberstadt, "The Soviet Economy: Worse Than We Thought," *New York Times*, November 23, 1988, for recent reports on the state of the Soviet economy.

20. Mary Kaldor, "Disarmament: The Armament Process in Reverse," in Weston (ed.), *Toward Nuclear Disarmament and Global Security*; Stanley Cohn, *Final Report to National Council for Soviet and East European Research: The Productivity of Soviet Investment and the Economic Burden of Defense*, State University of New York, Binghampton, July 11, 1983.

21. Rebecca Blank and Emma Rothschild, "The Effect of United States Defense Spending on Employment and Output," *International Labor Review*, November/December 1985.

22. Seymour Melman, private communication, February 3, 1988.

23. Mary Acland-Hood, "Military Research and Development," *Bulletin of Peace Proposals*, Vol. 17, No. 3–4, 1986; Dumas, *The Overburdened Economy*.

24. Marek Thee, "Science and Technology for War and Peace," paper prepared for the 29th Annual Convention of the International Studies Association, St. Louis, Mo., March 29–April 2, 1988; U.N. General Assembly, *Study on the Economic and Social Consequences of the Arms Race and Military Expenditures*; the remaining 5 percent of military R&D spending is mostly accounted for by Australia, Canada, India, Italy, Japan, the Netherlands, and Sweden; Barnaby, "Microelectronics and War"; The World Commission on Environment and Development, *Our Common Future* (Oxford and New York: Oxford University Press, 1987), for comparison with non-military R&D spending; Bischak's calculation is reported in Michael Dee Oden, *A Military Dollar Really Is Different: The Economic Impacts of Military Spending Reconsidered* (Lansing, Mich.: Employment Research Associates, 1988); for British share, see Mary Kaldor et al., "Industrial Competitiveness and Britain's Defense," *Lloyds Bank Review*, October 1986.

25. Organization for Economic Cooperation and Development (OECD), *Main Science and Technology Indicators 1981–1987* (Paris: OECD, 1988), Table 39; Ulrich Albrecht, "Rüstungsforschung und Dritte Welt," *Informationsdienst Wissenschaft und Frieden*, December 1984/January 1985, and Chander Uday Singh, "Here Comes the Juggernaut," *South*, November 1985, for military share of public R&D expenditures; Council on Economic Priorities (CEP), *Star Wars: The Economic Fallout*, (Cambridge, Mass.: Ballinger, 1988); National Science Board, *Science and Engineering Indicators 1987* (Washington, D.C.: U.S. Government Printing Office, 1987), and International Monetary Fund (IMF), *International Financial Statistics Yearbook 1988* (Washington, D.C.: 1988), for military share of government and private R&D spending.

26. Robert DeGrasse, "The Military and Semiconductors," in John Tirman (ed.), *The Militarization of High Technology*, for military-developed technologies; CEP, *Star Wars: The Economic Fallout*, and Kaldor et al., "Industrial Competitiveness and Britain's Defense," for share of applied research in U.S. and British R&D, respectively (by contrast, basic research accounts for more than 37 percent of civilian R&D programs sponsored by the U.S. federal government); Oden, *A Military Dollar Really Is Different*, for comparison of U.S. Navy and Department of Agriculture patents.

27. DeGrasse, "The Military and Semiconductors," for need to redesign; Hans-Peter Dürr, "Could Star Wars Work?" *World Press Review*, September 1985.

28. David Noble, *Forces of Production: A Social History of Automation* (New York: Oxford University Press, 1986); DeGrasse, "The Military and Semiconductors."

29. Simon Ramo, *America's Technology Slip* (New York: John Wiley & Sons, 1980).

30. United Nations, Department of Disarmament Affairs, *Economic and Social Consequences of the Arms Race and of Military Expenditures*, Disarmament Study Series No. 11 (New York: 1983), for global investment share; Dumas, *The Overburdened Economy*, for U.S. share.

31. Raphael Kaplinsky, "Guns and/or Butter: The Relationship between the Economy and the Military," *IDS Bulletin*, October 1985; Oden, *A Military Dollar Really Is Different*.

32. Cumulative military spending calculated from U.S. Department of Defense, *National Defense Budget Estimates for FY 1988/1989* (Washington, D.C.: Office of the Assistant Secretary of Defense (Comptroller), 1987). For human-made wealth and infrastructure repair needs, see Seymour Melman, "An Economic Alternative to the Arms Race: Conversion from Military to Civilian Economy," presentation at Rayburn House Office Building, Washington, D.C., November 1986.

33. Oden, *A Military Dollar Really Is Different*; U.N. General Assembly, *Study on the Economic and Social Consequences of the Arms Race and Military Expenditures*.

34. Executive Office of the President, Office of Management and Budget (OMB), *Historical Tables: Budget of the U.S. Government, Fiscal Year 1989* (Washington, D.C.: U.S. Government Printing Office, 1988), and *Economic Report of the President* (Washington, D.C.: U.S. Government Printing Office, 1988), for budget and trade deficits; Oden, *A Military Dollar Really Is Different*; National Academy of Engineering, *The Technological Dimensions of International Competitiveness* (Washington, D.C.: 1988), and DeGrasse, "The Military and

Semiconductors," for U.S. trade balance in manufactured and high-technology goods.

35. U.S. Central Intelligence Agency, *Handbook of Economic Statistics 1988* (Springfield, Va.: National Technical Information Service, 1988); IMF, *International Financial Statistics Yearbook 1988*.

36. U.N. General Assembly, *Study on the Economic and Social Consequences of the Arms Race and Military Expenditures*, for arms production value; Michael Brzoska and Peter Lock, *Rüstungsproduktion und Nuklearindustrie in der Dritten Welt, Militärpolitik Dokumentation*, Vol. 11, No. 59–61 (1987).

37. Ball, *Security and Economy in the Third World*; Clóvis Brigagão, "The Brazilian Arms Industry," *Journal of International Affairs*, Summer 1986.

38. Brigãgao, "The Brazilian Arms Industry"; Judith Vidal-Hall, "The New Arms Bazaar: Who Supplies the Matches?" *South*, November 1985.

39. Simcha Bahiri, "The Military-Industrial Complex and the Economy of Israel," unpublished manuscript, Tel Aviv, Israel, October 1987; Daniel Gavron, "Another Conversion Problem: Swords into Ploughshares," *Jerusalem Post*, January 17, 1989; Shlomo Frenkel, "Israel's Economic Crisis," *MERIP Reports*, October/December 1985; Brzoska and Lock, *Rüstungsproduktion und Nuklearindustrie in der Dritten Welt*.

40. Bahiri, "The Military-Industrial Complex and the Economy of Israel"; Esther Howard, "Israel: The Sorcerer's Apprentice," *MERIP Reports*, February 1983; Frenkel, "Israel's Economic Crisis."

41. Ball, *Security and Economy in the Third World*, Appendix 1, for composition of military budgets in selected Third World countries.

42. Ball, *Security and Economy in the Third World*.

43. "Military Inc.: The Armed Forces in Business," *South*, March 1988; Brzoska and Lock, *Rüstungsproduktion und Nuklearindustrie in der Dritten Welt*; Robert Springborg, "The President and the Field Marshal: Civil-Military Relations in Egypt Today," *MERIP Reports*, July/August 1987.

44. Johansen, *Toward a Dependable Peace*. Sivard, *World Military and Social Expenditures 1987–88*, for unmet human needs; Eisenhower quote is from his address to the American Society of Newspaper Editors, Washington, D.C., April 1953.

45. World Bank, *World Development Report 1988* (Washington, D.C., 1988), Table 23: Central Government Expenditure; on India, see "High Cost of Defense," *Economic and Political Weekly*, December 12, 1987; Ravi Rikhye, "Sleight of Hand," *The Illustrated Weekly of India*, December 4, 1988; Steven R. Weisman, "Ghandi's Arms Buildup Is Questioned at Home," *New York Times*, May 15, 1988.

46. "In 1971, the grant component of total U.S. military exports was 66 percent while cash sales and credit took up the rest. In 1979, the position had reversed dramatically. Only 5 percent of total U.S. arms transfers were in the form of grants while 61 percent were direct-cost transactions and 34 percent were financed by credit. . . . European countries have reduced the grant component of their arms transfers to an absolute minimum," according to Saadet Deger, *Military Expenditures in the Third World* (London: Routledge, Keegan Paul, 1986).

47. Rita Tullberg, "Military-related Debt in Non-oil Developing Countries, 1972–82," *Bulletin of Peace Proposals*, Vol. 17, No. 3–4, 1986; Michael Brzoska and Thomas Ohlson, "The Future of Arms Transfers: The Changing Pattern," *Bulletin of Peace Proposals*, Vol. 16, No. 2, 1985; Lloyd J. Dumas, "Economic Conversion: The Critical Link," *Bulletin of Peace Proposals*, Vol. 19, No. 1, 1988.

48. For an illuminating look at the implications of the debt crisis, see Susan George, *A Fate Worse Than Debt* (New York: Grove Press, 1988), and The Debt Crisis Network, *From Debt to Development: Alternatives to the International Debt Crisis* (Washington, D.C.: Institute for Policy Studies, 1985).

49. Sandra Postel, "Halting Land Degradation," in Lester R. Brown et al., *State of the World 1989* (New York: W.W. Norton, 1989).

50. Lester R. Brown, "Reexamining the World Food Prospect," in Brown et al., *State of the World 1989*.

51. Lester R. Brown, Christopher Flavin, and Sandra Postel, "A World at Risk," and Lester R. Brown, "Reexamining the World Food Prospect," in Brown et al., *State of the World 1989*.

52. Michael Weisskopf, "'Toxic Clouds' Can Carry Pollutants Far and Wide," *Washington Post*, March 16, 1988; Fernando Ortiz Monasterio, "Confronting Environmental Degradation: A Problem Without Borders," *Ceres*, September 1987; Hilary French, "Combating Toxic Terrorism," *World Watch*, September/October 1988; Patrick Smith with Alan George, "The Dumping Grounds," *South*, August 1988, for illegal waste dumping; Timothy Aeppel, "West Pays Price for Dumping on East," *Christian Science Monitor*, February 10, 1989, and Paul Lewis, "China Bids to Store Radioactive Waste," *New York Times*, February 8, 1984, for examples of officially sanctioned waste trade.

53. "Environment and Conflict," Earthscan Briefing Document 40, International Institute for Environment and Development, London, November 1984.

54. P.C. Mayer-Tasch, *Die Verseuchte Landkarte: Das Grenzen-lose Versagen der Internationalen Umweltpolitik* (Munich, West Germany: C.H. Beck, 1987); Thomas W. Netter, "Anger along the Rhine Grows After Chemical Spill," *New York Times*, November 12, 1986; "Swiss Accused by Bonn of Rhine Poison Negligence," *Financial Times*, November 11, 1986.

55. Joyce R. Starr and Daniel C. Stoll (eds.), *The Politics of Scarcity: Water in the Middle East* (Boulder and London: Westview Press, 1988); "Mighty Nile in Danger of Drying Up," *Populi*, Vol. 15, No. 3, 1988; Ghali quote from Lloyd Timberlake, *Africa in Crisis: The Causes, the Cures of Environmental Bankruptcy* (London: International Institute for Environment and Development, 1985).

56. Martin Wright, "Mixed Blessings of the Flooding in Sudan," *The New Scientist*, September 22, 1988, for Ethiopia; Jodi L. Jacobson, *Environmental Refugees: A Yardstick of Habitability*, Worldwatch Paper No. 86 (Washington, D.C.: Worldwatch Institute, November 1988), "Bangladesh Blames Neighbors for its Floods," *Panoscope*, December 1987, and Marvin Howe, "Bangladeshi Asks for Help on Controlling Floods," *New York Times*, October 11, 1988; Walter V. Reid, James N. Barnes, Brent Blackwelder, *Bankrolling Success: A Portfolio of Sustainable Development Projects* (Washington, D.C.: Environmental Policy Institute and National Wildlife Federation, 1988), for India; "Drowned by Politics," *The Economist*, September 17, 1988; Satanat Ali, "Stemming the Flood," *Far Eastern Economic Review*, October 13, 1988; Guo Zhongshi, "Anti-flood Cooperation with Bangladesh," *China Daily*, November 3, 1988.

57. Weisskopf, "Toxic Clouds Can Carry Pollution Far and Wide"; Emanuel Somers, "Transboundary Pollution and Environmental Health," *Environment*, June 1987; Norman Myers, *Not Far Afield: U.S. Interests and the Global Environment* (Washington, D.C.: World Resources Institute, June 1987).

58. Christopher Flavin, *Reassessing Nuclear Power: The Fallout from Chernobyl*, Worldwatch Paper No. 75 (Washington, D.C.: Worldwatch Institute, March 1987); "Czech/Austrian Nuclear Disagreement," *Financial Times European Energy Economist*, July 1, 1988; "Chilean Group Opposes Argentine Nuclear Waste Dump," *Ecoforum*, June 1988.

59. Cynthia Pollock Shea, *Protecting Life on Earth: Steps to Save the Ozone Layer*, Worldwatch Paper No. 87 (Washington, D.C.: Worldwatch Institute, December 1988).

60. Lester R. Brown, Christopher Flavin, and Sandra Postel, "A World at Risk"; Jacobson, *Environmental Refugees*.

61. Mayoom quoted in Lester R. Brown and Christopher Flavin, "The Earth's Vital Signs," in Lester R. Brown et al., *State of the World 1988* (New York: W.W. Norton, 1988); Worldwatch Institute, from U.S. Environmental Protection Agency, *Regulatory Impact Analysis*, Vol. 1 (Washington, D.C.: 1987), and from Matthew Wald, "Fighting the Greenhouse Effect," *New York Times*, August 28, 1988, for industrialized countries' shares of CFC and fossil fuel use; William K. Stevens, "Ecological Threats, Rich-Poor Tensions," *New York Times*, March 26, 1989.

62. The cost estimate is presented in detail in Lester R. Brown and Edward C. Wolf, "Reclaiming the Future," in Brown et al., *State of the World 1988*; Jonathan C. Randal, "Conference Ends at Odds on Pace of Ozone Efforts," *Washington Post*, March 8, 1989, for China and India's suggestion.

63. Wendell Berry, *Home Economics* (San Francisco: North Point Press, 1987).

64. Frederick Warner, "The Environmental Effects of Nuclear War," and R.P. Turco and G.S. Golitsyn, "Global Effects of Nuclear War," *Environment*, June 1988; Stockholm International Peace Research Institute (SIPRI), *Warfare in a Fragile World: Military Impact on the Human Environment* (London and Philadelphia: Taylor & Francis, 1980); Arthur H. Westing, *Environmental Warfare* (London and Philadelphia: Taylor & Francis, 1984); Knut Krusewitz, *Umweltkrieg: Militär, Ökologie und Gesellschaft* (Königstein, West Germany: Athenäum, 1985), for consequences of non-nuclear war; Olaf Achilles (ed.), *Natur Ohne Frieden* (Munich, West Germany: Knaur, 1988), for impact of peacetime military operations in West Germany; "Troubled DOE Facilities at a Glance," *PSR Monitor*, January 1989; Radioactive Waste Campaign, *Deadly Defense: Military Radioactive Landfills* (New York: 1988), for an overview of environmental problems linked to the U.S. nuclear weapons production complex.

65. World Commission on Environment and Development, *Our Common Future*.

66. On Rhine cleanup proposal, see John Tagliabue, "The Rhine Struggles to Survive," *New York Times*, February 15, 1987; on SO_2 inspection, see Volker Prittwitz, *Umweltaussenpolitik* (Frankfurt and New York: Campus Verlag, 1984); on Brazil, see Marlise Simons, "Brazil, Smarting from the Outcry over the Amazon, Charges Foreign Plot," *New York Times*, March 23, 1989.

67. Pollock Shea, *Protecting Life on Earth*, for Montreal Protocol; Samuel S. Kim, "The United Nations, Lawmaking, and World Order," *Alternatives*, Vol. 10, No. 4, 1985, for UNEP draft rules.

68. Michael Renner, *Rethinking the Role of the Automobile*, Worldwatch Paper No. 84 (Washington, D.C.: Worldwatch Institute, June 1988).

69. Sandra Postel, "Protecting Forests from Air Pollution and Acid Rain," in Lester R. Brown et al., *State of the World 1985* (New York: W.W. Norton, 1985); "European Nations Ratify Sulfur Reduction Pact," *World Environment Report*, September 17, 1987; Warren E. Leary, "Reagan, in Switch, Agrees to a Plan on Acid Rain," *New York Times*, August 7, 1988; "12 Nations Agree to Cut Pollution," *Washington Post*, November 1, 1988.

70. Hilary F. French, "Industrial Wasteland," *World Watch*, November/December 1988. Jürgen Vietig, "Ostblock Schlägt Europäische Umweltkonferenz Vor," *Süddeutsche Zeitung*, July 18, 1988.

71. Helmut Schreiber, "East and West Germany Cooperate to Control Pollution," *European Environment Review*, December 1988; Helmut Schreiber, Institute for European Environmental Policy, Bonn, private communication, March 17, 1989.

72. Schreiber, "East and West Germany Cooperate to Control Pollution"; "West Germans Look for Ways to Clean Elbe River, Seek Cooperation with East Germany, Czechoslovakia," *Multinational Environmental Outlook*, September 15, 1988; "East, West German Officials Struggle with Environmental Cooperation on Elbe," *Multinational Environmental Outlook*, August 4, 1988.

73. Prittwitz, *Umweltaussenpolitik*, for Rhine cleanup; "U.S. and Soviets Spur Scientific Collaboration," *Conservation Foundation Letter*, 1988:1, for SO_2 scrubbers.

74. William Echikson, "Hostile Neighbors Find Common Ground in Fighting Pollution," *Christian Science Monitor*, November 11, 1987; Jackson Diehl, "New Breeze in Soviet Bloc Is Fouled by Pollution," *Washington Post*, April 18, 1989; Swedish Embassy, Washington, D.C., private communication, April 7, 1989, for European Environment Fund proposal.

75. "U.S. and Soviets Spur Scientific Collaboration"; Cass Peterson, "U.S., Soviet Scientists Open Dialogue on 'Greenhouse Effect,'" *Washington Post*, May 12, 1988; "U.S., U.S.S.R. Scientists Join to Address Long-range Global Environmental Problems," *Multinational Environmental Outlook*, January 5, 1989.

76. John B. Oakes, "Greening Central America," *New York Times*, April 20, 1988; "Peace through Parks: A Proposal for Biological Reserves for the Protection of Unique Natural Areas on the Border between Nicaragua and Costa Rica," Nicaraguan Institute of Natural Resources, National Park Service of Nicaragua, Managua, mimeographed report, Spring 1986; "Peace Parks on the Rise," *IUCN Bulletin*, January/March 1989.

77. Philip Shabecoff, "Parley Urges Quick Action to Protect Atmosphere," *New York Times*, July 1, 1988, for Law of the Air proposal; Christopher Flavin, "Treaty Talks Begin on Global Warming," *World Watch*, March/April 1989, for climate change panel; Randal, "Conference Ends at Odds on Pace of Ozone Efforts," for CFC phaseout.

78. Permanent Mission of the U.S.S.R. to the United Nations, Statement of Eduard Shevardnadze before the 43rd Session of the U.N. General Assembly, September 27, 1988 (unofficial English translation); "Die Folgen des Wettrüstens für die Umwelt und andere Aspekte der Ökologischen Sicherheit," in *Tagung des Politischen Beratenden Ausschusses der Teilnehmerstaaten des Warschauer Vertrages, Juli 1988* (Berlin, East Germany: Dietz Verlag, July 1988), for Warsaw Pact communiqué.

79. For a look at grassroots action worldwide to reverse environmental degradation, see Alan B. Durning, *Action at the Grassroots: Fighting Poverty and Environmental Decline*, Worldwatch Paper No. 88 (Washington, D.C.: Worldwatch Institute, January 1989).

80. For Eastern European environmental movements, see French, "Industrial Wasteland,"; for Citizen's Treaty on Ecological Security, see Soviet-American Forum for Life with Human Rights, "Soviet-American Initiative Toward a Citizens' Treaty on Ecological Security and Human Rights," New York, undated, and Patricia Mische, Global Education Associates, New York, private communication, March 25, 1989.

81. For the full text, see "Convention on the Protection of the Environment between Denmark, Finland, Norway, and Sweden"; Lothar Gündling and Beate Weber (eds.), *Dicke Luft in Europa: Aufgaben und Probleme der Europäischen Umweltpolitik* (Heidelberg: C.F. Müller Juristischer Verlag, 1988), and Mayer-Tasch, *Die Verseuchte Landkarte*, for OECD proposal; there are a few cases in which courts have accepted the right of a foreign plaintiff to bring legal action against a domestic polluter: William Mahoney, "Geneva Appeals to Court in France to Block Restart of Nearby N-Plant," *Multinational Environmental Outlook*, January 5, 1989.

82. In retrospect, U.S. decisionmakers came to regret the decision not to ban MIRVs because Soviet land-based intercontinental ballistic missiles possess far greater throw-weights than U.S. ICBMs, enabling them to accommodate more warheads and thus use the MIRV-technology to greater advantage. For a detailed discussion, see Robert C. Johansen, *The National Interest and the Human Interest: An Analysis of U.S. Foreign Policy* (Princeton, N.J.: Princeton University Press, 1980), Chapter 2: "The Strategic Arms Limitation Talks."

83. Robert S. Norris et al., "START and Strategic Modernization," *Nuclear Weapons Databook Working Papers 87-2* (Washington, D.C.: Natural Resources Defense Council, 1987); a comprehensive curb on the strategic nuclear arms race would yield annual savings for the United States of approximately $40 billion, while a START treaty allowing modernization to go forward would save only about $6 billion a year; Michael G. Renner, "Disarming Implications of the INF Treaty," *World Watch*, March/April 1988.

84. On test ban verification, for example, see Robert L. Park, "A Bold Plan for Testing the Test Ban," *Washington Post*, January 22, 1989.

85. R. Jeffrey Smith, "Groups Urge Nuclear Arms Control by Limiting Production of Materials," *Washington Post*, February 26, 1989; Gabriel Schoenfeld, "A Secret Soviet Disaster?" *Washington Post*, March 5, 1989, for reports of possible problems in the Soviet nuclear weapons industry; Craig R. Whitney, "Gorbachev Plans to Stop Producing Uranium for Arms," *New York Times*, April 8, 1989; Matthew L. Wald, "Tritium Gap Called Path to

Arms Cuts," *New York Times*, December 11, 1988; J. Carson Mark, "The Tritium Factor," *Washington Post*, November 29, 1988.

86. For a brief account of these events and the text of the Joint Statement and the treaty outline, see Robert Krinsky, "An Introduction to Disarmament," Briefing Paper No. 2, National Commission for Economic Conversion and Disarmament, Washington, D.C., May 1988, and Lawrence D. Weiler, "General Disarmament Proposals," *Arms Control Today*, July/August 1986.

87. Marcus Raskin, "Draft Treaty for a Comprehensive Program for Common Security and General Disarmament," Institute for Policy Studies, Washington, D.C., July 1986.

88. Perhaps the best example of the refusal to rethink the fundamentals of security is the famous book by the Harvard Nuclear Study Group, Albert Carnesale, Paul Doty, Stanley Hoffmann, Samuel P. Huntington, Joseph S. Nye, Jr., *Living With Nuclear Weapons* (Cambridge, Mass.: Harvard University Press, 1983); Einstein quoted in Schell, *The Abolition*.

89. Sharp, *Making Europe Unconquerable*.

90. For a more detailed discussion of independent initiatives, see Robert C. Johansen, *Toward an Alternative Security System*, World Policy Paper No. 24 (New York: World Policy Institute, 1983); Mark Sommer and Gordon Feller, "'Independent Initiatives': Better Than Arms Control?" *New Options*, October 27, 1986; on 90-percent warhead cuts, see Johansen, *Toward a Dependable Peace*.

91. In response to strong public concern about nuclear fallout, the Limited Test Ban Treaty prohibited atmospheric tests but permitted underground explosions. The pace of nuclear testing remained unconstrained: about two-thirds of all nuclear tests conducted to date have taken place after 1963; "Simultaneous Test Ban: A Primer on Nuclear Explosions," *The Defense Monitor*, Vol. 14, No. 5 (1985); Stockholm International Peace Research Institute, *SIPRI Yearbook 1988* (Oxford, United Kingdom: Oxford University Press, 1988).

92. For Gorbachev's initiatives, see Renner, "Disarming Implications of the INF Treaty"; Jerry W. Sanders, "America in the Pacific Century," *World Policy Journal*, Winter 1988–89; William M. Arkin, "Gorbachev Talks but Who Listens?" *Bulletin of the Atomic Scientists*, March 1989.

93. For a good analysis of the evolving European situation, see Michael Lucas, "The United States and Post-INF Europe," *World Policy Journal*, Spring 1988; a detailed presentation of proposals for a non-offensive defense is given in a set of articles in *Bulletin of the Atomic Scientists*, September 1988.

94. Mary Kaldor, "Beyond the Blocs: Defending Europe the Political Way," *World Policy Journal*, Fall 1983; Mark Sommer, *Beyond the Bomb* (New York: Expro Press, 1985); Harry B. Hollins, Averill L. Powers, Mark Sommer, *The*

Conquest of War. Alternative Strategies for Global Security (Boulder, San Francisco, and London: Westview Press, 1989).

95. Hal Harvey, "Defense Without Aggression," Bulletin of the Atomic Scientists, September 1988.

96. Bernard E. Trainor, "Soviet Arms Doctrine in Flux: An Emphasis on the Defense," New York Times, March 7, 1988, Paul Lewis, "Soviet Offers to Adjust Imbalance of Conventional Forces in Europe," New York Times, June 24, 1988, and Dmitri Yazov, "The Soviet Proposal for European Security," Bulletin of the Atomic Scientists, September 1988, for "reasonable sufficiency" concept; Soviet Embassy, Washington, D.C., Press Release, "Mikhail Gorbachev Addresses the United Nations," December 8, 1988, and "In Gorbachev's Words: 'To Preserve the Vitality of Civilization,'" New York Times, December 8, 1988, for Gorbachev's U.N. speech; Charlotte Saikowski, "Warsaw Pact Rushes to Trim Troops," Christian Science Monitor, February 8, 1989, and David Remnick, "Gorbachev Says Military Budget Faces Cutbacks," Washington Post, January 19, 1989, for Warsaw Pact military cuts; see Tagung des Politischen Beratenden Ausschusses der Teilnehmerstaaten des Warschauer Vertrages and Michael R. Gordon, "Cutting Arms in Europe: It's Down to the Details," New York Times, March 9, 1989 for Warsaw Treaty proposal at conventional arms talks.

97. Frank Barnaby, "The Nuclear Arsenal in the Middle East," Technology Review, May/June 1987, and Spector, "New Players in the Nuclear Game," for recent proliferation evidence; Robert C. Johansen, "Non-progress in Non-proliferation," Sojourners, September 1980.

98. "The Requirements for Stable Coexistence in United States-Soviet Relations," Congressional Record, May 9, 1988.

99. Philip Taubman, "Gorbachev Offers Disputed Radar for Peaceful Exploration of Space," New York Times, September 17, 1988, for Gorbachev bases-trade proposal.

100. Hilary F. French, "Restoring the U.N.," World Watch, July/August 1988.

101. "A U.N. Office Looks to Prevent War," New York Times, April 16, 1989; Paul Lewis, "Soviets Say U.N. Peacekeeping Effort Should Emphasize Prevention," New York Times, October 18, 1988.

102. Nicaragua's proposal from Johansen, "The Reagan Administration and the U.N.: The Costs of Unilateralism," World Policy Journal, Fall 1986; Honduras's proposal from Wilson Ring, "Honduras Holding U.S. Responsible for Contras," Washington Post, October 23, 1988; Robert Pear, "Central America Negotiates on Its Own," New York Times, March 19, 1989, for tentative peacekeeping force; Pentagon estimate from Joanne Omang, "Policing a Latin Peace Projected to Cost Millions," Washington Post, May 11, 1985; U.S. spending from Joshua Cohen and Joel Rogers, "Central America Policy:

The True Cost of Intervention," *The Nation*, April 12, 1986; Central American spending from ACDA, *World Military Expenditures and Arms Transfers 1987*.

103. Robert C. Johansen, "For a Permanent U.N. Police Force," *Christian Science Monitor*, October 13, 1982.

104. For 1988, expenditures totaled about $250 million; the sum of $380 million is arrived at by annualizing the initial three-month cost of keeping U.N. observers in Iran and Iraq ($37.5 million), based on George D. Moffett III, "Peacekeepers Win Peace Prize," *Christian Science Monitor*, September 30, 1988.

105. Torleiv Orhaug, "An International and Regional Satellite Monitoring Agency," in Joseph Rotblat and Soen Hellman (eds.), *Nuclear Strategy and World Security* (London: MacMillan, 1985); cost estimate is reported in United Nations, *Economic and Social Consequences of the Arms Race and of Military Expenditures*.

106. John Tirman, "International Monitoring for Peace," *Issues in Science and Technology*, Summer 1988; Owen Thomas, "Nations Keep an Extra Eye on Each Other," *Christian Science Monitor*, September 28, 1988; "Shevardnaze Offers New Arms Plan at U.N.," *Surviving Together*, Summer 1988; for the Canadian proposal, see "PAXSAT Concept: The Application of Space-Based Remote Sensing for Arms Control Verification," Verification Brochure No. 2 (Ottawa: Canadian Department of External Affairs, undated); for text of Representative Robert Mrazek's bill, see H.R. 4036, "The International Security and Satellite Monitoring Act of 1988," introduced on February 29, 1988 (the bill was reintroduced in the 101st Congress on March 22, 1989, and hearings are planned for 1989); personal communications with Robert Katula, special assistant to Robert Mrazek, October 3, 1988, and March 22, 1989.

107. Johansen, *Toward a Dependable Peace*.

108. Seymour Melman, *The Demilitarized Society* (Montreal: Harvest House, 1988); in 1984, for example, the U.S. Census Bureau reported that 10 of the largest arms industries realized on average a 25-percent return on equity compared with an average return of 12.8 percent for other manufacturers; Inga Thorsson, "Disarmament and Development: An Idea Whose Time Should Have Come," *IDS Bulletin*, October 1985.

109. See H.R. 101, "The Defense Economic Adjustment Act," 101st U.S. Congress, introduced by Representative Ted Weiss; for a discussion of the bill's main provisions, see Jonathan Feldman, Robert Krinsky, and Seymour Melman, "Criteria for Economic Conversion Legislation," Briefing Paper No. 4, National Commission for Economic Conversion and Disarmament, Washington, D.C., December 1988.

110. Jonathan Feldman, "An Introduction to Economic Conversion," Briefing Paper No. 1, National Commission for Economic Conversion and Disarmament, Washington, D.C.: May 1988; Herbert York, "Some Possible Measures for Slowing the Qualitative Arms Race," *Proceedings of the 22nd Pugwash Conference on Science and World Affairs*, Oxford, U.K., September 7–12, 1972 (Oxford: 1973).

111. ACDA, *World Military Expenditures and Arms Transfers*; "Military Plant Goes Civilian," *China Daily*, November 23, 1987; "China Invents the Entrepreneurial Army," *Economist*, May 14, 1988.

112. "In Gorbachev's Words," and Remnick, "Gorbachev Says Military Budget Faces Cutbacks," for arms production cut.

113. Hal Harvey, "The Best Defense is Dealing with the Roots of Conflict," *New Options*, No. 38, April 30, 1987, for an advocacy of improved efficiency as a means for reducing conflict; Lloyd J. Dumas, "Economics and Alternative Security: Toward a Peacekeeping International Economy," draft manuscript, University of Texas (Dallas), 1989.

114. George F. Kennan, "After the Cold War," *New York Times Magazine*, February 5, 1989.

MICHAEL RENNER is a Senior Researcher with the Worldwatch Institute and coauthor of *State of the World 1989*. Prior to joining Worldwatch, he was a researcher at the World Policy Institute in New York and a Corliss Lamont Fellow in Economic Conversion at Columbia University. He is a graduate of the University of Amsterdam, where he studied international relations.

THE WORLDWATCH PAPER SERIES

No. of Copies*

_____ 30. **The Dispossessed of the Earth: Land Reform and Sustainable Development** by Erik Eckholm.
_____ 31. **Knowledge and Power: The Global Research and Development Budget** by Colin Norman.
_____ 33. **International Migration: The Search for Work** by Kathleen Newland.
_____ 34. **Inflation: The Rising Cost of Living on a Small Planet** by Robert Fuller.
_____ 35. **Food or Fuel: New Competition for the World's Cropland** by Lester R. Brown.
_____ 36. **The Future of Synthetic Materials: The Petroleum Connection** by Christopher Flavin.
_____ 38. **City Limits: Emerging Constraints on Urban Growth** by Kathleen Newland.
_____ 39. **Microelectronics at Work: Productivity and Jobs in the World Economy** by Colin Norman.
_____ 40. **Energy and Architecture: The Solar Conservation Potential** by Christopher Flavin.
_____ 41. **Men and Family Planning** by Bruce Stokes.
_____ 42. **Wood: An Ancient Fuel with a New Future** by Nigel Smith.
_____ 43. **Refugees: The New International Politics of Displacement** by Kathleen Newland.
_____ 44. **Rivers of Energy: The Hydropower Potential** by Daniel Deudney.
_____ 45. **Wind Power: A Turning Point** by Christopher Flavin.
_____ 46. **Global Housing Prospects: The Resource Constraints** by Bruce Stokes.
_____ 47. **Infant Mortality and the Health of Societies** by Kathleen Newland.
_____ 48. **Six Steps to a Sustainable Society** by Lester R. Brown and Pamela Shaw.
_____ 49. **Productivity: The New Economic Context** by Kathleen Newland.
_____ 50. **Space: The High Frontier in Perspective** by Daniel Deudney.
_____ 51. **U.S. and Soviet Agriculture: The Shifting Balance of Power** by Lester R. Brown.
_____ 52. **Electricity from Sunlight: The Future of Photovoltaics** by Christopher Flavin.
_____ 53. **Population Policies for a New Economic Era** by Lester R. Brown.
_____ 54. **Promoting Population Stabilization** by Judith Jacobsen.
_____ 55. **Whole Earth Security: A Geopolitics of Peace** by Daniel Deudney.
_____ 56. **Materials Recycling: The Virtue of Necessity** by William U. Chandler.
_____ 57. **Nuclear Power: The Market Test** by Christopher Flavin.
_____ 58. **Air Pollution, Acid Rain, and the Future of Forests** by Sandra Postel.
_____ 59. **Improving World Health: A Least Cost Strategy** by William U. Chandler.
_____ 60. **Soil Erosion: Quiet Crisis in the World Economy** by Lester R. Brown and Edward C. Wolf.
_____ 61. **Electricity's Future: The Shift to Efficiency and Small-Scale Power** by Christopher Flavin.
_____ 62. **Water: Rethinking Management in an Age of Scarcity** by Sandra Postel.
_____ 63. **Energy Productivity: Key to Environmental Protection and Economic Progress** by William U. Chandler.
_____ 64. **Investing in Children** by William U. Chandler.
_____ 65. **Reversing Africa's Decline** by Lester R. Brown and Edward C. Wolf.
_____ 66. **World Oil: Coping With the Dangers of Success** by Christopher Flavin.

*Those Worldwatch Papers not listed are out of print.

_____ 67. **Conserving Water: The Untapped Alternative** by Sandra Postel.
_____ 68. **Banishing Tobacco** by William U. Chandler.
_____ 69. **Decommissioning: Nuclear Power's Missing Link** by Cynthia Pollock.
_____ 70. **Electricity For A Developing World** by Christopher Flavin.
_____ 71. **Altering the Earth's Chemistry: Assessing the Risks** by Sandra Postel.
_____ 72. **The Changing Role of the Market in National Economies** by William U. Chandler.
_____ 73. **Beyond the Green Revolution: New Approaches for Third World Agriculture** by Edward C. Wolf.
_____ 74. **Our Demographically Divided World** by Lester R. Brown and Jodi L. Jacobson.
_____ 75. **Reassessing Nuclear Power: The Fallout From Chernobyl** by Christopher Flavin.
_____ 76. **Mining Urban Wastes: The Potential for Recycling** by Cynthia Pollock.
_____ 77. **The Future of Urbanization: Facing the Ecological and Economic Constraints** by Lester R. Brown and Jodi L. Jacobson.
_____ 78. **On the Brink of Extinction: Conserving The Diversity of Life** by Edward C. Wolf.
_____ 79. **Defusing the Toxics Threat: Controlling Pesticides and Industrial Waste** by Sandra Postel.
_____ 80. **Planning the Global Family** by Jodi L. Jacobson.
_____ 81. **Renewable Energy: Today's Contribution, Tomorrow's Promise** by Cynthia Pollock Shea.
_____ 82. **Building on Success: The Age of Energy Efficiency** by Christopher Flavin and Alan B. Durning.
_____ 83. **Reforesting the Earth** by Sandra Postel and Lori Heise.
_____ 84. **Rethinking the Role of the Automobile** by Michael Renner.
_____ 85. **The Changing World Food Prospect: The Nineties and Beyond** by Lester R. Brown.
_____ 86. **Environmental Refugees: A Yardstick of Habitability** by Jodi L. Jacobson.
_____ 87. **Protecting Life on Earth: Steps to Save the Ozone Layer** by Cynthia Pollock Shea.
_____ 88. **Action at the Grassroots: Fighting Poverty and Environment Decline** by Alan B. Durning.
_____ 89. **National Security: The Economic and Environmental Dimensions** by Michael Renner

_____ **Total Copies**

Bulk Copies (any combination of titles) **Single Copy** $4.00
2–5: $3.00 each   6–20: $2.00 each   21 or more: $1.00 each

Calendar Year Subscription (1989 subscription begins with Paper 88) U.S. $25.00 _____

Make check payable to Worldwatch Institute
1776 Massachusetts Avenue, N.W., Washington, D.C. 20036 USA

Enclosed is my check for U.S. $ _____

_____
name

_____
address

_____
city   **state**   **zip/country**

*Those Worldwatch Papers not listed are out of print.

four dollars

Worldwatch Institute
1776 Massachusetts Avenue, N.W.
Washington, D.C. 20036 USA